ISBN-1484171063
ISBN-13: 978-1484171066

Different!

By

Leslie Hammond

Preface

Different has been written to provide an explanation of an individual person's, cross dressing experiences. As of today, there is no logical reason or answer as to why men like to dress in ladies clothes.

The person concerned is actually the author, who has gone to great lengths to express his feeling which understandably, 'wax and wane' from time to time. He delayed writing certain parts of the book until his feelings and desires returned, enabling him to best express how he felt at that time. These 'feelings' that returned are expressed in *Italic* text. You'll be able to pick out when his interests have waned which are written in normal text.

All the events are true from best memories. Name and places have been omitted in order not to cause perhaps embarrassment or identity for those concerned.

Introduction

As a man who's had the desire to dress in ladies clothes for many years, I felt it important to be able to share my experiences with others who, perhaps have the same desires or, who have just a curious nature and want to understand a little more of this subject which is, often surrounded by a certain mystery.

Equally important, I felt the need to explain my feelings toward others and how important it is to respect other's thoughts on this subject and, for those wives and partners who often struggle to understand this desire. The burning question "why do you want to dress in ladies clothes?" is dealt with in order that some explanation can be concluded and, for those contemplating to dress, to give some thought for what you actually want to achieve.

As our modern world becomes a smaller place and we learn more of each other's cultures and habits. It's a fact that there is huge number of men who do dress up in ladies clothes and, there is an even larger number who have the desire to. For the man who has these feelings the question, "should I?" is a difficult one and can play on a man's mind for many years and even cause depression and mood swings. Given that the subject is to say the least, of a very sensitive nature, the feeling and desire is often put to the back of his mind, however one thing is for certain, it never actually goes away!

Writing this book from a man's perspective obviously brings a bias view on the subject. This being recognized, I've gone to great lengths to consider the feelings of others and, to respect their opinions. It will be up to the reader to draw his/her conclusion on the subject, however if it provides some more understanding of what makes a man want to dress in ladies clothes and, bring us perhaps a little near to understanding why, then my many hours sat behind this key board will have been worthwhile.

Chapters

Chapter 1

What's right and what's wrong?

Now, starting to write a book and titling the first chapter, What's right and what's wrong?, is to say the least, a 'tall order'. However, I believe that in every walk of life, if you understand the basics, then these ideals stand you in good stead for the rest of your life. When I refer to the term 'basic's', I refer to the common law and family virtues for which, I've been brought to understand and respect and, that has provided a country where law, order and discipline has set the standards for most successful countries of the world. Without them, we're nothing!

Yes, as you'll have guested, I'm British and extremely proud of both our Queen and Country. As the world has developed over the years, our systems, laws and cultural awareness and understanding had been the role model for others to use. It's without doubt that we've made some mistakes, however we've learnt by them and continue to support ethical and cultural understandings which, provides the stability for most other developing counties aspire to achieve.

Often when reading a book, particularly an autobiography or a personal account, I find it somewhat a little frustrating only to find after you're half way through the book, the person who you perhaps admired or, aspired to be like has some traits or tendencies that bring you to conclude 'this person is not the person you thought he/she was' and, somehow reading on is a waste of time as you're not going to agree with his/her doings in future chapters. You're probably thinking what has all this got to do with men's desires to dress in ladies clothes, a lot!

If you research the subject either through reading a book, internet or seeing a TV program, men dressing in ladies clothes is usually associated with some sort of sexual desire, either to change their identity in order to further their relationships [usually with other men] or, they have feeling so strong that they actually wish they'd been born a woman. Each and every individual is different and our feelings, emotions and desires vary considerably.

My feelings and desires over the years are quite straight forward and uncomplicated. I'm a man in every aspect of the word, a true male straight forward guy with, a liking to dress in ladies clothes from to time. Reaching the age of fifty nine years, I've had a remarkable life, in fact a life that many people could only dream of and, I've enjoyed every part of it. Yes, there have been peaks and troughs, highs and lows, however that's life! Without the lows, there'd be no highs and we should be contented and understand this.

Coming from a stable family upbringing with good parents and, living in an ideal location for a child to grow up in, and having interests in many varied aspects of life enabled me to meet up with the most wonderful woman in the world, my wonderful wife. Our life together has, been a picture book story right through to today and, I've no doubt in my mind that it will continue forever and 3the day. We have two wonderful children and now a grandchild too, and so many other wonderful things in life, and I'll share with you, as we get further into this book.

Some people say, I'm lucky, fortunate and others say "it's alright for you". I'm sure you've heard these comments from time to time especially when you've bought or achieved something perhaps a little out of the ordinary. While perhaps there is a certain element of luck in this life, in mine there has been a lot of hard work and sacrifice, dedication and a burning desire to make a success of what I like doing most, and that is helping others to succeed. No one has handed me anything on a plate and there's nothing wrong with handouts! Everything, what I'd done before we were married and after, has taken a lot of effort to achieve and we're proud of this, as our children. Proud of the fact that we have adhered to life's basic disciplines and rules, proud of the fact that we have passed these important virtues to our children who in the same way as we have, embracing and enjoying them in every way.

We don't compromise on the basics of our life in anyway, they are important. Life is full of fun and wonderful things and, enjoying each day as it arrives and all of the simple things around you is truly a blessing! Somehow, the more advanced we become as human race, the more complex life becomes and we see ourselves becoming more and more reliant on materialistic items. There is no going back from here for anyone and, the developing world wants the same, its human nature and again, we should embrace the good and enjoy. There is however a price to pay for such a life and, the stress that it brings. People deal with stress in many different ways and, in many cases chose to do something which is against the basic virtues and laws of our society and in some cases, chose to abuse them and undermine the very fabric of life, which is, the marriage between and man and woman.

Dealing with emotions and stress is something we all approach differently and mostly, we stay on the 'right side of life'. There are those who wish to move over to the wrong side of life and choose to break the law by taking drugs, theft and other wrongs doings. Crime is something I've zero tolerance for and, for anyone who choses deliberately to do wrong or, to inflict pain and suffering to others. Seeing a person being arrested is a pitiful sight as in many circumstances, they release they have done wrong and, are coming up against the strong arm of the law. They know they have done wrong, however to avoid accepting the consequences of the error of their ways, they chose to tell lies and try to get out of it. Theft and robbery is more rampant in the developed world than the third world countries. Some people believe they have a given right to have material items or money, without having to make any sacrifices other than, to plan to seal them from others. There are those who chose to abuse the rights and happiness of others due to the fact that they for whatever reason feel deprived believes they rightfully should have what others have worked for.

Life is simple and, should remain so. Living an uncomplicated life is easy and reaching a point whereby, you can feel contented is a huge achievement. Enjoying the basics of life and seeing all of the wonderful things that surround you is something we all often overlook and, it's mainly due to the modern way of life that has unfortunately become the norm. We tend to rush around and try to get so much done and in many circumstances, have no other choice if we are to pay bills and, perhaps please a wife or partner. It all brings pressure, stress and unnecessary emotions which build up and, if not dealt with in some way or other, can lead to unhappiness and even depression. Our lives should remain enjoyable and rewarding. Learning to deal with the stresses of life is something we all have a different approach to and, there is no perfect solution as to how we deal with it. One thing is for certain though, knowing what is right, what is wrong and staying on the "right side of the line" is important to us all.

I make this point simply because, a man who chooses to dress in ladies clothes can more often than not, even if he's a good straight forward law abiding citizen become branded as someone who's "crossed the line" and is doing something wrong. It's a fact that if the subject if brought up in conversation or perhaps prompted by a news release or, just someone's observations, a man dressing in ladies clothes is somehow associated with an illicit sex act or, some weird pervert hanging around public toilets and even a child molester! Unfortunately, people always see the 'dark side' of the subject and this presents totally the wrong impression for what really if is nothing other than, the enjoyment of materials and clothes. Strange, but it's true! How far does a man take his dressing desires? It's an individual choice. However, there are certain considerations that have to be taken into account before furthering a perhaps 'life times' desire, as the consequences if they go wrong, can be devastating.

Referring to "what is right and what is wrong" is something I make reference to often in the coming chapters as I believe, if these can be understood by everyone, wives, lovers, partners and whomever you wish to share your desires with [that is if you are planning too or currently do], may provide a better understanding of this simple yet, complex subject.

Chapter 2

Why do I want to dress?

t's the million dollar question everyone asks! "Why does he want to dress in ladies clothes?" or, "why do I want to dress in ladies clothes?" If you can answer either of these two questions, you'll become a very wealthy person and, a much admired person as you'll finally provide a conclusion for men who long to have an answer and more so, for those loved ones who wonder why?

There are countless articles on the subject and many theories, however one thing is for sure, there is no answer. It remains a mystery and to this day, even the most qualified while they provide endless papers and debates on the subject, still they don't come to the conclusion, why? Given that there is no answer to the questions, it all adds to the subject which, is open for many opinions and debate. When I refer to a man who has the genuine desire to dress in ladies clothes, I mean just that, and not to be confused with a man who's looking for some sort of extension to his sexual desires. Please understand that I've no wish to talk about a man's sexual desires and his relationships, those are an entirely different subject and something I've no wish to discuss or to write about.

My interest in wearing ladies clothes is just that, to wear and enjoy the clothes and the materials they're made from. Too feel the sensation of being dressed in ladies clothes and, to admire the end result. That's my preference and nothing more. Dull? Boring? Well, maybe I am but, that's me and I wouldn't change anything for the world! You may well decide that reading any further will not full fill your expectation and bring satisfaction that you're looking for. Whatever your interest, the fact remains that men are attracted to ladies, it's a natural way of life, however to want to wear their clothes and dress up as a lady is perhaps something a little different, unique and in many people's eyes and, just simply intolerable in others! So, recognizing that you too, may be interested in some form of dressing, it's a fascinating subject and I hope you'll become a little more aware of the pros and cons of the subject. If you do want to dress, it's also important to understand how far you wish to go.

My desire goes back from a very early age for which I have many fond memories and, I'll share these with you in the coming chapters. Perhaps you to have had the same experiences or, later in life it's just a feeling that has somehow materialized and you're not too sure how, when or why, it just happened. The desire has been with me for fifty years, and I can't to this day say why I have this feeling, I just do.

The feeling comes and goes and can stay away for days, weeks, months and even years then one day, it's back and I've asked myself on countless occasions, "what triggered that off?" There's never an answer and I know only too well that as I type this paragraph, I've no wish at the moment to put an ladies clothes on and, I've no idea when the feeling will next be with me. However, one thing is for certain, it will come again! I've leant to deal with it and to be happy and contented with my thoughts. When the feeling comes over me, it's a happy one and something I enjoy to think about.

My career has involved me with engineering and I've travelled the world working in many exotic countries, and had the privilege to meet and work with some wonderful people of many different cultures, backgrounds and religions. It's been and still, is a wonderful experience and helping others perhaps less fortunate than myself and giving people a chance to 'have a go' and make a success of their life is my real reward. Now you'd never associate a man who has been involved with engineering, heavy equipment, mining, ships, engines and a whole spectrum of a typical man's world, to have the liking for wearing ladies clothes, however I do! Men who wear steel toe cap boots with overalls and who work in oily conditions. Who put up with immense heat and even danger, all fall into the typical mould of what a man should be. This is me, though in later years my I've swapped my boots for polished brown leather brogue shoes and my overalls have been replaced with pressed trousers and crisp white shirt and tie. Engine rooms have been replaced with board rooms and airplane seats, hotel rooms and a life of email and meetings. However one thing is true, I'm still very much a man, living in man's world, dealing with men and enjoying everyday challenges as they present themselves. Who would think that this man equally, likes the feel of wearing stretchy knickers and nylon stockings, high heeled shoes and a full cup bra? I do.

Do I have a preference of being dressed as man or a lady, no!

If you asked me today would I be interested to go shopping and chose some new clothes, the answer would be no! At the moment it really doesn't interest me at all. If the feeling isn't there then there's no point as it would be like shopping for a set of paint brushes when you've no use for them. I can walk through a department store and pass the ladies clothes and lingerie section without even thinking or having a second glance at what's on display. Indeed, I can be shopping with my wife and perhaps she see's something that she'd like, such as a blouse or skirt and she'll often ask for my opinion. I'm only too pleased to offer advice and like to pick clothes up that I think would suit her and spoil her from time to time. You would ask "wouldn't you prefer to be buying that for yourself?" and the answer is simply no!

It doesn't even enter my head to think about ladies clothes when I have no feelings for the subject, then suddenly from nowhere it just arrives returns. Perhaps I can be driving our car, watching TV, having a shower or mowing the grass and I know it's returned again. What does it feel like? Well that's difficult to describe, however it's a warm and comforting feeling that I know I'd like to dress up in ladies underwear. Was it something I eat or, was it something I was thinking about that triggered it? Never an answer, it just happens. I've given many hours of thought as to what triggers my feeling off, but never come up with an answer. It just arrives and can stay with me for an hour, a day, week and longer. It's even arrived and I've felt good about the feeling and thought as soon as the opportunity arrives I'll dress. However, sometimes only an hour later and thinking, 'what shall I wear?' suddenly I realize that the feeling has gone and I've about as much interest in dressing as watching paint dry! My interest has gone and even to the extent sometimes I feel silly to have even thought about getting dressed, 'why would I do that?' It comes, it goes and I've learnt over the years that no matter what I try and do, it's going to be with me for the rest of my life.

Does this upset me, no!

I'm more than happy to understand these are my personal feelings and thoughts. It gives me a feeling of completeness

10

inside to know, that I've mastered this blessing [or curse] which ever it is and, perhaps I'm lucky to have figured out how to deal and manage these feelings with a sense of joy and contentment. For many men, they have the urge and desire to dress but never actually take the plunge and put on something that they fancy wearing. It's there, in their mind but they don't actually bring this to reality. Some are happy with that, they leave it as a fantasy while others agonize of the decision and can't quite make the move for perhaps fear of being found out and looked upon as a sissy or not knowing what it's going to feel like to wear perhaps a pair of knickers or a bra. They might not like it and their feelings and long kept desires could end in disappointment. For others perhaps the feeling of wearing some clothes would become a compulsion and they may then want to wear them all of the time. This could lead them to think, do they really want to go down this road and where would it end?

So much to think about and it's only a simple subject, clothes, materials, what am I making such a big deal about?

Is it right or wrong to wear ladies clothes and enjoy the feelings and desire? That's for you to decide and try to answer. For me, it's quite simple, so long as it's not going to harm yourself and, more importantly others, then why not?

Yes, these feelings have been with me since an early age when I didn't understand the facts of life and, all of the implications that wearing ladies clothes would bring, however I've dealt with the subject. It's a mind set from that age and can say, one I've been happy with ever since. Did I ever tell anyone during those early years? No! Did I ever think that perhaps I should tell someone? It crossed my mind but whom? If I'd of told my palls in school for certain they would have laughed at me, no point in sharing my feelings there! If I was to tell my Mum, would she understand, would she be cross and even disappointed with me? Perhaps she would have been, so I preferred not to tell anyone and keep the subject to myself. Perhaps I could have told the doctor, however in those days the doctor was only called when you were ill and couldn't attend school, so there was never an opportunity to tell him and, what would he have thought?

He'd probably of immediately discussed the subject with my mother and asked what she knew about it? That wouldn't' have been fair so, as I say just kept those feeling to myself and, I have been happy to do so all of my life. I've always thought that perhaps I have some feelings that are unique to me and felt perhaps quite privileged in knowing that I have a liking for ladies clothes and the desire to dress up from time to time.

Has this feeling ever made me think perhaps I'd like to dress like a lady for full time? No definitely not!

Do I ever wish I'd been born a girl, and could have grown up as a lady and be able to wear ladies clothes as the norm, all of my life? No, definitely not. I'm a man and enjoy being a man in every sense of the word. Being a husband, a father, lover and friend, I wouldn't change that for the world! I'm fully aware and sympathize with men who feel everyday they should have been born a female. That must be a really difficult feeling to deal with as you must know, that the whole man way of life just doesn't suit you and every day, is one of frustration and agony. That must be a difficult 'cross to bear' to speak and for these men, they have my sympathy.

For those men who have this constant feeling and know full well they are prepared to sacrifice their male way of life to gain some piece of mind, and be able to enjoy a female way of life, they deserve to have what they aspire to be. It must take a huge courage and conviction for an individual to reveal his feelings and want to have the necessary operations to bring them as close as they me become to physically looking like a woman. I don't believe however, no matter how much surgery and man goes through; they will ever become a true woman as the mind of a woman is different to a man. For certain, it will provide that 'piece of mind' they have been looking for and, enable them to live the life of a man who has under gone extensive surgery enabling them to live their life as they desire. It's should bring contentment and, a life as close to being a woman as possible. Contentment is extremely important in this life. If you don't have or are failing to achieve the happiness and contentment you're looking for, then it's time to stop and have a really long think, 'where am I going and, what do I want?" are the questions a person should ask themselves.

For me I'm happy to be a man and, wouldn't want to change anything.

There are men who have the desire to dress in ladies clothes to full fill some fantasy that they have perhaps dreamt up or read about that, sex with a lady may feel even better, if they dress in ladies clothes! It's an individual choice and not something that 'lights my candle' so to speak. I've no desire to discuss men's fantasies as for certain, it's an entirely different subject. We all have our own inner thoughts and feelings, likes and dislikes, desire and even loathing's, however these I believe are personal and I'm not the sort of person who shares such feelings and thoughts. As for those who do, well it's their choice; however I believe they should really keep these within the circles in which they mix and not for the general public.

Today more than ever as we have the wonderful internet at our finger tips, you can search any subject you like. Just type anything you wish into Google and its spit out many options for you to further your enquiry. Type in the words 'men dressing an ladies clothes' and the results are endless, indeed you'd either fall asleep or just simply be unable to open and read all of the results. One thing is common though, if you are a man who dresses in ladies clothes for whatever reason, you're put into a category and named either, a transvestite or a cross dresser. There are other name and titles, however these mainly relate to their sexual orientation or desires. Again, I've no wish to discuss or enter into a conversation about this subject. My reason for righting to book is not to share or discuss my thoughts and sex life, those are personal and that's the way they will remain. Some men get a great kick out of discussing their sexual desires and even, their recent sexual affairs with friends. Perhaps they see it as a way of demonstrating that they have an attraction that women can't resist, and it makes them feel that they are the perfect sort if man that every woman has a desire for. There may be a certain element of truth in this, however and once again, that's for you to decide.

If, as the internet and all of its pages suggest, I'm to be categorized with one of these names, then I believe the title 'cross-dresser' is fitting for me. Do I like this title? I've no problem with this as it's true to say, I dress in man's clothes and from time to time in ladies clothes, so the term 'cross dressing] seems fitting for me.

Do I find my feelings and desires toward dressing in ladies clothes somewhat kinky or sex related? No, not at all! Perhaps for those who look to wear ladies clothes as an extension of their sexual fantasy will find this difficult to believe, however my desires have never lead me to feeling like that. Perhaps this is where I [and may be many other men also] feel that my desires to wear ladies clothes is put into the 'sex and weirdo basket' due to the fact that most men who have these sexual fantasies. Some want to further them seem and want to have the public know about it in some form or other. This I believe is where the main issue and problem area arises in particular for a loved one, wife or

14

partner who struggles to understand this desire of their partner. Even with all of the trust in the world, it brings about the underlying question of 'why does he want to dress in ladies clothes?' The fact that the man they married or live with was in every sense of the word 'their man', now suddenly has the liking for wearing ladies clothes. It automatically connects with sexual desires and, leads to the thought 'what is he thinking about and isn't our sex life good enough?'

Obviously even for the most open and trusting relationship, it would bring about questions that need answers! The whole subject of a successful marriage or partnership is based on love and trust. Both go hand in hand and, one will never work without the other. To bring such a question into this relationship automatically brings about some suspicion which is something that should never be permitted to happen. Again, it's a difficult subject to even discuss as it's somehow tainted with the sexual and weirdo thing [so to speak] and for this the majority of people in this world they have no desire to want to discuss or, understand it. It's seemed wrong in many people's minds and in many cases, it is wrong. That being said we are all different and there are circumstances that have lead people into situations perhaps by accident or by design where they seem to feel that what they are doing is 'cool' [as I believe is the modern term]. We seem to have become a more forgiving nation I recent years however, on that same note we are more critical of one and other than ever before. This has been brought about through the exposure of men who chose to further their sexual desires and pray on children and young boys and girls. The days of standing at the school gate as father and handing out sweets to the children as they go home or to catch the bus, are frowned upon. Even to be seen helping perhaps child and in particularly, a little girl immediately casts suspicion as to your motive and sadly enough, these thoughts seem bias toward you being a molester, or some sort of pervert.

Somehow, the public link these type of 'horrible doings' with men who perhaps are somehow a little different from the norm and, if you are known to wear ladies clothes then definitely you're recognized as possibly being one of these persons.

This whole subject really turns my stomach and I have zero tolerance for any man or woman for that matter, who chooses to take advantage of children. No matter how they are analyzed and the 'do gooders' of this world who always try and see the other side of the coin, for me it's a complete no no! End of story. The wellbeing of children and trust they place in adults is all part of their perfect innocence and to abuse that, there is no excuse what so ever.

Again, as I make all of these points, I'm pleased to share my experiences and thoughts with those who chose to read this book and it may well help you in your decisions, whatever they may be as your life continues. In summary, 'why do I want to dress?' truthfully I've no answer and, I believe there is no answer. It's one of life's little mysteries and will remain so.

The fact that I gain a degree of satisfaction, comfort, warmth and contented feeling is what I experience through dressing. We are all different and perhaps other men with the same desire and who actually dress, feel the same. As the subject is somehow deemed to be bordering on the weird side of life, most men don't talk about it, they don't bring it up in conversation and therefore not a lot is known about the subject. I've communicated with some likeminded people over the years on the internet and discovered I'm not alone with my special feelings and they too feel the same. Their biggest worry and sleepless nights are mainly to try and explain to their wives, why they want to have a go in ladies clothes and wish she would understand his desire. The fear of upsetting someone close to you can be a huge burden, I know as I too, have had this challenge over the years. It's not easy and the desire to dress can be looked upon as either a blessing or, a curse!

Chapter 3

Dressing from an early age

When you start to ask the question what really makes me want to dress in ladies clothes and why, as with most analyses you start to look back at the past in order to try and figure out when it started. Some times this can be a difficult task and not everyone has as good a memory or, even choses to remember their past. For me it's crystal clear, and I can recall things from my childhood that are as though they only happened a few months ago. That being said, I've not a good memory for facts and figures in particularly at work. Being able to quote percentages and actual figures off the top of your head is always very foolish as from the time when you lasted looked at such data, things could have changed and you could be providing the wrong information effecting a critical decision. Better to refer to the updated facts and present them as found, not 'as you thought!' When attending an interview with BP Shipping many years ago to become a junior engineer officer, one thing that was drilled into me that I've never forgotten was, don't try to remember any facts, write them down as was the point of providing a top pocket in your overalls, a pen and note book! Wrong information could lead to a wrong decision and result in a disaster for the vessel or ship resulting in a loss of life! Your mind has enough to think about, keep facts where they belong and provide correct data when it's required not, 'I think so!'

My memory for my early life is somewhat remarkable. I believe this is attributed to having a wonderful up bringing with fond memories that I can recollect in detail. For certain, I don't get every detail right, however for the benefit of the details in this book, I've checked names and people's characters with others who knew them and, the good thing is their thoughts and recollections are the same as mine! Incidentally I've not shared the fact that I'm writing this book with anyone other than my wonderful wife, and I'll explain the reasoning for this later.

As a youngster at the age of five and six years of age I was totally fascinated by the railways and the steam locomotive and like most other children and boys of my age, we all wanted to be an engine driver or a stoker! Train spotting was my main hobby for many years and I've very fond recollections of stations, signal boxes, guards vans, foot plates and a host of other locations I was privileged to be in when train spot.

Obviously my hobby and interest lead me to want a model railway at some point and for a treat on holiday once, we visited what seemed like a huge model railway layout in Llandudno. It was located in the main street up above a shop and I was just totally engrossed! My father too liked railways and used them extensively to travel for his work as he worked away returning home on a 'once per month' bases and always used the train.

As Christmas would loom with all of the excitement, I wanted a train set and there were a few good toys shops in our area, both of whom they stocked Hornby Doublo and Triang railways. Obviously I'd take every opportunity to look in the shop windows and even to go and ask if I could have a look

19

at a certain loco. I really enjoyed that hobby and even today, I have a great interest in railways and really enjoy the opportunity to visit preserved lines and travel in carriages from the past pulled by steam locos, they're just brilliant!

In this era, the early sixties, the catalogue shopping was born or at least, it came to our part of the world. This entailed someone becoming a local representative and coordinating all sales for which they would receive a commission. It must have been a nice little earner for those who wanted to supplement their income. The catalogue would be given to a house hold for a week or two during which time you could have a look at all of the goods and select what you wanted to purchase and, either pay for it outright or, pay monthly installments which eased the load on the weekly / monthly salary or wages. It was in fact a credit facility; though somehow back then it wasn't looked upon for this purpose, more a way of being able to shop at home and, have the items you selected delivered to your door.

I'd told my Mum & Dad this particular year that I'd very much like a train set for Christmas and it arrived all wrapped up, it was exactly what I wanted and I can remember the countless hours spent setting it up and playing with it on the front room floor. At that age I lived on the floor whether watching TV, listening to the wireless as it was known then or just simply playing with Dinky toys or, my train set.

Obviously when you have a train set its good fun to make things like tunnels and see the train and carriages disappear at one end and reappear at the other. Making mountains out of cardboard boxes with glue and paint was good fun and, obviously to need for more rolling stock was a must. The catalogue had a good selection of Triang Railways and I used to spend hours looking at these when lying on the floor. The catalogue was filled with a great variety of items from clothes to toys, from garden tools to bikes and all sort of wonderful items. Compared with today's internet and Argos they must have seemed like the future and, it worked well. I'm not sure if we still today have catalogue shopping as we knew it then, however some of the long established companies are still trading which makes me think perhaps they could be.

Back then at an early age, I'd browse through the pages and dream 'of all of the thing's I'd like, if we had lots of money' or as my Mum & Dad would say, 'if we win the pools!" Clothes seemed to take up the biggest space in the catalogue and mainly ladies, these seemed somehow boring though as a youngster, I'd do all sorts of things like look at every page just so that I could say, 'I've seen every page in the book'. The ladies underwear section always seemed to have many pages and it fascinated me very much to look at the very different underwear that was available for them and how little available for boys and men. There were pictures of ladies wearing different underclothes and I was intrigued to know why? The way in which they had long socks and the way which they held them up were interesting and, the types of clothes they used. This was all new to me and I wanted to know more, and would take the opportunity to study the pages in the catalogue.

I'd make sure that my Mum was either deep I to her knitting or watching TV and I'd look through the pages of underwear which to this day, I find fascinating. Fascinating to the extent I want to wear and feel them on my body! Yes even at that early age!

While looking at these fascinating clothes, I couldn't really understand what they were for and, why men didn't have the same types of clothes because in the men's section, their clothes were similar to those in the boys section. Ladies dressing in these fascinating underwear garments was a real intrigue for me and somehow I became interested at that early age and wanted to learn more. Perhaps you would say that's strange for a boy the age of eight years, however it's true and I knew then that something inside me had me hooked on this subject, however at that age I didn't really know what.

Looking at ladies in bras, I began to understand that a ladies chest was different to mine, different to a man's as, and we didn't have those 'bumps on the front' like ladies do. It never crossed my mind to think what those 'bumps' were for and why ladies had them. I guess that was the innocence of youth! Somehow they looked good and also I liked the different lengths they came in, as some went right down and covered the ladies bottom. Others just had a strap around their back and over their shoulders. At that time the only colours that were in the catalogue was white or pink. There were many pages of ladies knickers too, mainly normal size ones and some with longer legs. These really fascinated me and, I wondered why men didn't have the same type of clothes.

Ladies as I leant from the pictures didn't have the same type of socks as men either, in fact they were quite different in so much as they were a lot longer and came a long way up their legs. These where held up in place with sort of straps and clips which I presumed must have been put there to stop them falling down. For some years, I would look at the pictures with a fascination and, from time to time there would be adverts in the Sunday newspaper for ladies clothes. I used to notice these as for a few years I delivered papers on a weekend, filling in for the full time paper boy. These adverts again where fascinating and kept my interest in this subject and, made me even more inquisitive. Please understand that, I kept this to myself and was happy with the knowing that somehow I had this feeling that gave me a 'comforting feeling' knowing that I very much liked ladies underwear!

It's perhaps not easy to understand that a boy of that age should have such an interest, however I did and other than the fact I was fascinated with these under clothes and the certain mystery that surrounded them, I never questioned in my mind if it was the right or wrong thing to think about them as it wasn't harming anyone and, who knows, other boys could have been thinking the same, only we never told one and other.

I'd be about nine or ten years old when I was asked by my school pals if on Saturday, I'd stand in as goal keeper in a football match they were having as the goal keeper was off with Chicken Pox. I'd no interest in football at all. Cricket was good fun and 'rounders' too, but football I found boring. Anyway, they kept asking me and said I'd only have to stand in goal and not to worry about doing anything else so, I agreed. The game was all planned for the morning at the playing field and my friend lent me some football boots and gloves. I'd already got shorts and shirt which I used for PE in school. So, I got changed at home and headed off across the fields to the match. When I arrived there, the guys were practicing and gave me lots of advice, not that I really intended to put it in to action, though somehow I didn't want to let them down. The match started and our team was winning, in fact the ball hardly came over to my end of the pitch due to their good playing. It came on to drizzle with rain and the pitch soon turned muddy, especially in goal as the grass had worn away with lots of use. The second half saw the opposition try harder and the ball came over to our end of the pitch more often. Watching, I could see that one guy who had the ball was really focused to try and score a goal finally took a shot. It was my chance to show that I was part of the team and save the ball from entering the goal! I'd no idea how to save the ball and just jumped over and the ball hit me and then bounced on the ground. I dived over and managed to shield it from the other players and, actually save the game! It was a moment of pride, though I'd still no interest in football but was pleased to have done my bit to help my friends. As I kicked the ball as hard as I could toward our players, the ball sored into the air and again, I was quite taken back with the power in my kick. After that, things went quiet for the rest of the game and the ball didn't return to my end of the pitch. Then the whistle blew and the game was over. By this time that cold wet and muddy feeling was all over me, and the rain was pouring down. Everyone quickly grabbed their bags and disappeared as did I. Crossing the fields on the way home, I called in at the local corner shop where my Mum worked. She was serving someone and I told her we'd won the game for which she seemed pleased and, told me to get home and have a warm bath as I looked cold and she didn't want me to catch a chill.

The shop was only a few streets away from our house so I ran home soaked to the skin and found the back door key in the usual hiding place and unlocked the door to the porch. Walking inside I was like a drowned rat and dripping wet and muddy. To save making a mess through the house I took all of my clothes off in the porch, it had frosted glass so no one could see in and there was no one else at home. Wiping my feet on the mat, I went through to the bathroom, put the plug in the bath and ran some hot and cold water. It didn't take long to fill enough for me to have a warm bath and, it was good! I was cold and dirty and the warm water was really welcoming. I washed off all of the dirt and mud and rinsed myself off. It would have been nice to have a soak for a while, but the water wasn't such a nice colour so I stood up and again rinsed myself and pulled the plug out. The water drained away and I dried myself on a nice warm towel as the radiator in the bathroom was always on and, the towels always nice and warm. With all of the water gone, I turned on the cold tap and ran lots of water to rinse down the dirt until the bath was clean and then turned the water off.

Just as I was finishing drying myself, I noticed something sticking out of the wash basket and my curiosity got the better of me. I opened the lid to see more of what it was. It was one of those ladies clothes used for holding up those long socks and had those clips on the ends of the straps. I recognized it from what I'd been looking at in the catalogue and it was an experience I'll never forget. I was actually holding one of those clothes that I'd been fascinated to look at for some year previous. I sat on the side of the bath and wondered how you would wear it and what it was really for as it seemed quite a big thing, just to hold those long socks up. It had an opening on one side with lots of hooks an eyes and a small bow on the waist band at the top on the front. It was made from a sort of stretchy elastic type material and was white in colour.

By this time I was so fascinated that I wanted to 'have a try on' just to see what it would feel like. It was late in the afternoon and I was the only one home so just in case someone arrived home, I shut the bathroom door and slid the lock. By this time I was starting to tremble with a feeling of excitement of actually holding a piece of clothing I'd been looking at for some time, and here it was in my hands! As I'd still not dressed after having my bath I put the garment around my waist and tried to fasten the hooks, but it kept sliding off me. I fastened them all on the floor then pulled it up over my legs and tummy. The feeling was just unbelievable! Even thought it was a bit too big for me, here I was standing wearing this wonderful garment which had six straps dangling from the bottom sides. The feeling of elastic and the slight pulling on my tum was just something that has stayed with me until today.

I looked in the wash basket again and sure enough, there were some of those long thin socks and I picked these out and had a good look at them. These too felt strangely good and I put one on my leg and had a go at fastening it to the strap. I couldn't quite figure it out at first but soon realized how they worked and fastened the remaining two, then I put on the other sock and fastened that one also. The whole experience was just a feeling that I still have today when putting on similar clothes, it's never left me and I feel pleased to have had such an experience so early on in life.

When dressed for the first time, my thoughts were, "I wonder what I look like?" and wanted to have a peep in the mirror. The only mirror which would work was the one in my Mum & Dad's room, the front bedroom of the house. I was very conscious of the fact that someone could arrive home at any time didn't want to risk getting caught in these new found clothes. We had a small shaving mirror which stood on the bathroom windowsill, so I used that as best I could and was just amazed at what I saw. Me, dressed in some ladies clothes, clothes you never see or hear anyone talk about, it was exciting and I was really delighted to say the least at being able to 'have a dress up'. As time was passing, I took off the socks and the garment and placed them back in the wash basket just as I had found them, and closed the lid leaving only the same strap sticking out. I unlocked the door and went to my bedroom and got dressed. It was perhaps a more luck than judgment not to have gone to use the mirror in the front bed room as, just as I was coming out of my room I heard my Mum arrive home shaking her umbrella. She called to me to ask if I'd had a good warm bath for which I replied, 'yes I've only just come out' and my mother replied saying she was going to have one, as her walk home in the rain had made her feel cold.

That evening there was only the two of us in the house as Dad was working away and my brother, was staying over with friends. With the fire stoked up and a nice warm front room, we both settled into watch TV with me taking my pride of place on the floor and looking at the catalogue knowing that I'd tried on some of those ladies clothes. After reading up on the items, I leant I'd been wearing a white, side hook and eye fastening girdle with six suspenders and, a pair of tan coloured nylon stockings. While I was interested to learn more and obviously understanding that the clothes I'd tried on belonged to my mother, I never thought to go through her dressing table draws and see what else she had as somehow, I believed this to be wrong. It would have been like looking through someone's personal things which I didn't and still today, don't think is right.

It was some years after when I next had the opportunity to wear ladies clothes again, on the odd occasion when I remembered, I'd have a quick look in the washing basket, however there were no such clothes waiting for the wash. It never bothered me either as I somehow knew that one day, I'd have the opportunity to dress again and perhaps, in more easy surroundings.

It was some years later at the age of twelve when my next dressing up session happened and it was totally unplanned. I'd still from time to time look through the catalogue when we'd have a one to look at and also, I'd look in the Exchange and Mart magazine as they to use to advertise ladies clothes for sale. My interest came and went and it never became an obsession of any sort. Somehow, I was just happy in knowing 'I'd had a go' and would at some point have another go to enjoy the experience and feelings of warmth and comfort it brought to me.

I'd been out delivering milk as I'd had a new Saturday job which involved early starts, something I've always liked. It was winter time and I'd been out with the deliveryman and we'd had some lunch, collected a few outstanding milk monies and then called it a day. It was cold and he dropped me off at the corner shop where my Mum was still working. I told her we'd finished for the day and was heading home. She told me that she'd loaded the fire, so the house would be warm and she'd see me later as there was only the two of us for tea. Similar to before, Dad was working away and my brother was stopping over with his cycling palls. I walked home and changed from my milk delivery clothes and had a warm bath with intentions to settle in by the TV and watch the Saturday afternoon sports. Running a bath I jumped in and had a good soak then pulled the plug and reached across to the towel rail for a warm towel. It was just right, warm and comforting and I proceeded to dry myself when, something caught my eye. It was similar to that some years ago, an item of ladies clothing hanging out of the wash basket.

I dried myself off and had a peep to find this time some stockings and a smaller belt type garment with those straps, similar to those on the previous garment I'd tried on before. This was a suspender belt and had the same hook and eye fastenings, this time at the back. Looking again in the wash basket there were several pairs of stockings and I couldn't wait to have a try on. I knew my mother wouldn't be home for at least a couple of hours and as it was getting dark, I wrapped my dressing gown around me and proceeded to draw all the curtains in the house, as this was a ritual that my Mum did in the winter, to keep the place as warm as she could. Once done, I turned the key in the back door, just in case anyone called. Back to the bathroom and took off my dressing gown and put on the suspender belt. It felt wonderful with the six straps dangling against my legs. I'd grown since last trying on clothes and this time they fitted better. I pulled up and rolled on the tan stockings and

28

fastened them to the suspender clips, oh how exciting was this. Also in the basket was a bra, this looked interesting and I took it out and tried it on. The feeling was delightful if those are the correct words, truly delight full and something again I'll never forget.

I dressed, in the bathroom just in case anyone arrived home even though I'd locked the door, just in case. As the curtains were all drawn, I felt the need to have 'look at myself', so I crossed the hall to the front bedroom and put on the light. There stood in front of the mirror and looked at me, dressed in ladies underwear and it felt really good, exciting and pleasing! I stood there for a few minutes and admired the view. I could have stood there for ages, however time was passing so I switched off the light and was making my way back across the hall toward the bathroom when there was a loud 'rat tat tat' on the front door! There was no curtain over the door and I froze, more with fright and being startled. I stood there dressed in these clothes and couldn't move for what seemed like ages until I decided to make a dive for it, and shot behind the hall cupboard. Immediately the letter box opened and note dropped on the hall mat. I was to say the least, in panic mode as what if someone had seen me? What if someone had seen me dressed in ladies clothes? I can't tell you how awful I felt!

Waiting for a minute, I stood up and went to the bathroom and changed out of those ladies clothes and put everything back as it was, then went to my room to get dressed. I tried to relax but somehow was on edge to think, someone might have looked through the letter box when pushing the note through and spotted me. Mum arrived home later and started to make our evening meal and asked me if anyone had called. I said I'd heard someone while I was in the bath and that they had put a note through the door. Handing it to her, she opened it and said it was from the lady who organized

29

our catalogue and it was a note say she'd called but as there was no one in, however she'd put the catalogue in the coal house. I was sort of relieved and went outside and sure enough, there was a new catalogue in plastic wrapping propped up in the coal house. I brought it in side and my Mum said we could have a look through it later in the evening.

Quite by chance, she'd brought home some shopping for a friend of hers who lived in the next avenue and asked me if I'd mind popping it around for her, as she'd not been well and couldn't get out for her shopping. No problem, I put on my jacket and got my bike out and proceeded to ride off to the lady's house. Just turning the corner I nearly bumped into someone rushing across the road and we both stopped and apologized. It was the lady who had put the note through our front door! My heart was racing as if she'd seen me, then she would be sure to say. She was a nice sort of lady and said 'I've been to your house this afternoon but there was no one in so, I left a catalogue in the coal house for you'. I said I was in the bath when you called and found your note and the catalogue later. She said that she was pleased and hoped we'd enjoy looking at it then wished me good night. Had she seen me? No I don't think so as for certain, she would have said something.

That evening I spent quite some time looking through the new catalogue and enjoyed looking at the larger than ever selection, of ladies underwear and dreaming of all of the items I'd like to try on! From that time onward, my feelings and desires to dress came and went and, never bothered me as I knew what a wonderful experience it was to wear such fantastic clothes, ladies clothes, and ladies under clothes that not many people talked about. It felt unique. Somehow, I felt and always have felt privileged to have this enjoyment and experience that perhaps many men would like to do, but never somehow have the courage or perhaps more so, the opportunity to do so. The images in that mirror, gave me many hours of comfort. Yes me, dressed in ladies underwear, how wonderful it felt, the materials, the clinging sensation and the feeling of being all strapped up somehow was indescribable.

Snap shots of the catalogue pages that attracted me to ladies clothing from an early age. Nothing has changed! My feelings are just the same!

Chapter 4

Blessing of a curse?

Life brings about many opportunities and challenges. It's all part of what makes living in this wonderful world a pleasure if only we can recognize it. Modern life in comparison to the older way of life which was perhaps harder, in many ways due to the lack of modern amenities and appliances, it was in many ways simpler and slower. Today life is fast and only becoming faster. The world is becoming a smaller place. Overseas travel is becoming the norm for more and more people and with the development of the internet, affordable communications are becoming more and more available to everyone. The tradeoff for all of these modern conveniences is the fact that the pace, at which we live our lives, is accelerating rapidly and even simple things like sitting around the table and enjoying an evening meal or dinner together is, becoming a rarity!

We have so much to achieve and so many places to visit. All too often, we take for granted what we actually have around us and for use of a better term, get quite blinded as we often, 'we can't see the woods for the trees'. Sometimes it takes an illness, or other such unpleasant circumstance for us to stop and take stock, too look around and realize what we have is wonderful and, start to enjoy every day and all of the wonderful things within our grasp as opposed to striving for the unreachable all the time.

Contentment in your life brings a whole new meaning to the enjoyment of everyday things you have. Things you can see, touch and feel be them leaves and grass, friends and family, people in general and most of all, your health and wellbeing of others around you. These are some of the most important things in life and, if you can stop and 'take stock' as they say, look around and realize that while perhaps you don't have the latest car, the best house in the street, you have yourself, perhaps a partner, wife, children and even more, your health. These are the important things in life. Giving is much more important that receiving it is said and, I can say this is very true. One of my biggest buzzes is helping people who are less fortunate that myself, who perhaps never had the chance to 'have a go and prove themselves'. If I can provide that chance, then it really is a rewarding feeling.

Having feelings of your own can bring a huge amount of satisfaction, happiness and contentment. Feelings that you're starting to enjoy every day simple things, contented to help others around you and realize that you're 'not to badly off after all' really bring a new dimension in this busy world in which we live. Listening to the birds in the trees, the wind howling around the chimney pots on a wet winter's night and knowing you're all warm and snugged up in bed for instance is one of the most satisfying feeling, there is. Nothing compares somehow. It's a unique feeling and, costs nothing just needs a few moments to experience and realize these are the good simple things in life that you can enjoy if you take the time, to do so.

For many years after getting married, our lives seemed to accelerate faster and faster and, all for the good as we were getting on with our lives, bring up a family and enjoying as much as possible in those special away from work together moments. One thing though and my wife made me aware of was the fact that I was always striving for the next goal without evening stopping to draw breath and look at what we'd already achieved. It was true and somehow I struggled to come off that compelling 'treadmill, fast lane of life' until one day I woke up and thinking what she had said to me time and time again, I actually stopped and looked around. It was one of the most magical moments of my life when I realized, I have so much, much more than many others only hadn't taken the time to appreciate it.

When I actually stopped and started to think about things, simple things that I'd been taking for granted and not even enjoying, life became even more pleasurable and, for this I'm beyond words to say the right ones that can convey my thanks to my wonderful wife. If you read this my dear, "thank you!"

The desires a man has for dressing in ladies clothes can bring so much contentment, so much happiness and satisfaction if they can only be realized. I've mentioned that men dress for a variety of reasons, for the reasons other than my own it's not possible for me to make comments and say what is wrong or right, it's for you and the individual to make their own 'what they will out of it'. For me and by now I hope you're starting to understand what it is about dressing I like and enjoy, this feeling brings so much inside happiness and joy. To actually put those desires into practice and slip on a pair of stockings, to breath in and fasten those girdle hooks and eyes, to pull those laces on my corset gives me even more pleasure, more satisfaction and a feeling of contentment. To me it's a blessing that I actually have these desires and feelings. To be able to express myself in front of the mirror and see the shapes I create and feel the materials either swishing against my legs, or to be all bound up holding my stomach in a new found shape is just wonderful. Again, for me these feelings are a blessing, though I'm very aware of the fact that for some, they can be a curse.

For many men, in fact I would think by far the vast majority who, have a desire to dress simply don't because they either don't get the opportunity or, have mixed feeling about them putting on some knickers of whatever garment takes their fancy. It can plague many men for their entire lives and, leads to all sorts of problems such as mood swings, grumpiness and generally having the feeling of dissatisfaction within their lives. And this can be regardless if position or wealth, it's something they know they would like to try and, just haven't taken the time to do so. In some cases they never will and live with the hidden desire which they can and do cope with. For others, it nags at them day in, day out and plagues their thoughts each time, ladies underwear of the type of clothes they desire come in sight. What is for me and many others is a blessing, for many men it's a curse.

Many men actually are frightened to admit that they have this desire for fear of being found out as it would hurt their male ego. It's a fine line between holding a male ego in front of friends and letting it go to admit too themselves, they quite fancy putting on some satin knickers! Can you imagine if, one of their colleagues or friends was to find out? It would bring their ego tumbling down and that's something they couldn't handle. In this case usually, men prefer to try and keep it in the back of their minds. However one thing is for sure, if you've had this desire or thoughts once, they will reappear. Why? No one knows and again, hopefully if some reads this book who is well versed on this subject just may find something that could help them bring some many theories to a conclusion.

Wives and lovers, friend and partners would all breathe a sigh of relief if they could only understand the simple answer to this question. I too, would really like someone to be able to provide me with the answer! It easy to for us all to judge without understanding the true story, and it's just the way we are, however, giving some consideration to those who do dress and trying to provide some help and guidance, is something I really feel would help many men better come to terms with their thoughts. I'm not for one minute suggesting that every wife, partner or whoever's concerned should immediately agree with a dressing habit, no definitely not! However if any progress is to be made with gaining a better understanding, then it's no good just brushing it under the mat, it would be better brought out in the correct surroundings and given the time it needs to be explained. I've never explained these feelings to anyone only my wife and, that took some doing believe me!

It's been a long time in the coming out, however I took the plunge and broached the subject in order to try and somehow explain this desire and feelings I have. If at any time, I felt that this would have posed a threat to us in anyway, I'd of never have brought the subject up. It's a fine line to tread as for certain, and for all of the reasons I mention in this book, it can upset even the most patient and understanding lady from all of what I've read on the subject. How else would it be possible to talk about, to explain about it, to share my deepest thoughts? Somehow, it's like being torn between a rock and hard place as the saying goes, you're dammed if you do and, you're dammed if you don't. It's not that I expected her to agree and say "that's ok dear, you carry on", far from it as I knew she'd have concerns and, I wanted as part of my explanation to try and alleviate those concerns. Only then would I be able to try and see how and if, there would be any possible way for us to deal with this together or not.

If I said, the world would be a happier place if men could somehow relieve themselves of this strange desire, I feel sure that hundreds if not thousands of men, would pay a small fortune to make this happen. To relieve the burden of what they carry around, and even the closest person to them doesn't know. To be able to bring it out in the open without fear of being laughed at or even persecuted would be a wonderful step forward. Will this ever happen, well may be if men like myself who are prepared to write about the experience, the desire, the reasons they feel the need to dress, only then will we stand half a chance of understanding more. Blessing or a curse, what's it for you?

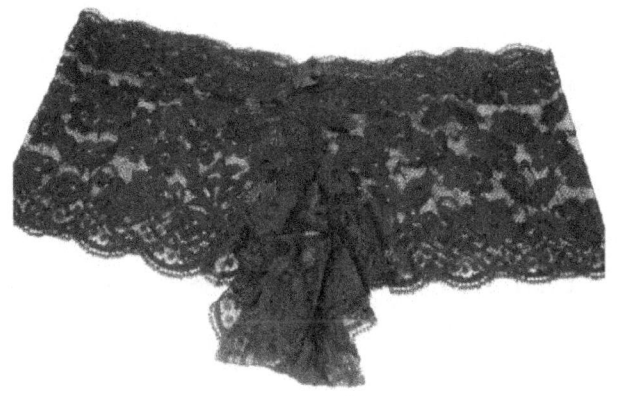

Chapter 5

Is there something wrong with me?

A s you can imagine, having had me thoughts, and desire to dress from any early age and keeping these very much to myself, from time to time I'd question myself and ask 'is there something wrong with me?" The answer I've always concluded is simply, no. I'm a man who lives a perfectly normal life and enjoys all of the wonderful things that it presents on a daily bases. The fact that I like the touch and feel of a satin blouse as much as a clean crisp white shirt is perhaps even a gift that many men don't possess. In fact it's a privilege in many ways and something I'm proud of.

I have friends who are into cycling and truly get a biz out of wearing their thin body hugging 'lycra' cycling gear. They say they're both comfortable to wear and feel nice against their skin. The feeling of having material that appeal to you, next to your body makes for a pleasing sensation and, much this comes down to your approach and attitude of enjoying all of the good things around you. While perhaps many other people in their daily rigours of life put on clothes just as 'the norm' and, something to wear without even questioning, 'does this look nice and moreover, does it feel nice' is perhaps something they are overlooking and missing out on. Wearing nice clothes is something I very much appreciate and this doesn't mean I spend a fortune on clothes and always have the latest styles. On the contrary, many of my clothes have many years of use and I make sure they are looked after and in good condition, if they start to look a little worn or tired, I replace them. Men's socks are perhaps one of the most boring presents that a man can receive at Christmas time it's reported in media magazines; however I find nice socks a delight! I always like long socks that are stretchy and cling to my feel and legs and somehow get a lovely feeling when pulling them on. Similarly I enjoy rolling a nylon or silk stocking on my leg and making sure my toes and heel are comfortable with no twists or anything that would make them feel uncomfortable. Both are a delight to put on and have next to my feet and legs, both have the same purpose and, from as far back as I can remember, they both have and still give me enjoyment. These are just some of the simple things in life which people over look. When I refer to people, I mean both men and women.

In recent years with the equality of men and women coming more and more prevalent, many women are choosing to dress in less feminine styles and seem more focused to comfort and perhaps practicality. Obesity is having an effect on the way women dress and I find it quite concerning to see younger women who seem to have lost all sense of pride in the way they dress and choose to wear track suit pants and tops as these stretch and are easy to wear in accommodating their expanding shapes. They really must have lost all dress sense as if they were to take five minutes and look at themselves in the mirror, I just wonder if they would actually see themselves as other see them. For them, shape wear and maintaining a smart appearance seems to have been forgotten or, perhaps their up brining was such they their parents didn't offer any assistance or guidance toward maintaining a smart and presentable appearance. It's a shame as for certain with some help and supports their interest in themselves and their appearance would soon bring them to realize with a little care and dedication, they can transform themselves back to what they all really want to look like, smart and attractive!

It doesn't mean to say that a woman with an overweight, full figure is going to look like a cat walk model, far from it but learning to dress properly brings that all important confidence back, "look good, feel good!" The once person who I greatly admire is Gok Wan. This man has brought so much pleasure to so many women. It's really quite amazing to see the look of enjoyment on their faces as he provides his make-overs and transforms them into a new person. He somehow has the very clever way of making even the most nervous of women confidence in themselves in order to 'take the plunge and dress in what he recommends which in some cases can be quite different from what they believe suits them.

He's very cost conscious and takes everyday 'high street' shop clothes and adds his magic touch transforming even an unexciting style I into a cat walk special. There is something special in his approach which is quite outspoken in many ways and gains their confidence within minutes. He never holds back when describing a ladies body and provides suggestions and more often, outfits transform perhaps a 'saggy and bulging' figure to become very attractive and an appealing shape. Look good, feel good is my wife's motto which she taught me many years ago and, it's true!

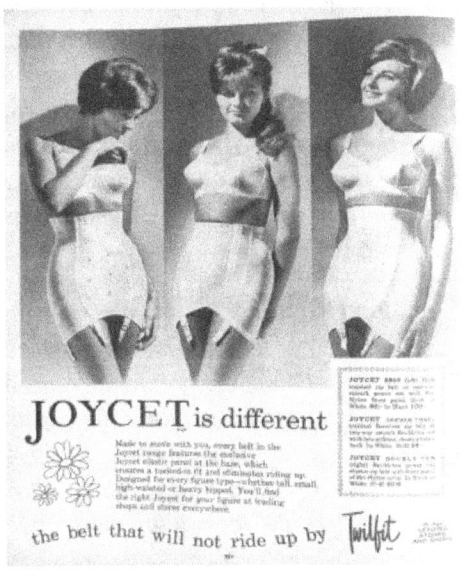

JOYCET is different

the belt that will not ride up by Twilfit

Chapter 6

Childhood influences

Of the many books that have been published on the subject, there is often mention that perhaps childhood influences had some baring on men who, later as they grow in life have the desire to dress in ladies clothes. It's a very good point, and something I want to share with you in order that, perhaps my experiences had an influence on my desires. It may just be coincidence, it may have nothing to do with why all of the years I like ladies underwear and other clothes.

There are questions regarding a person's make up even though a baby is born either male or female and certainly we know that some men actually feel so strongly that they are a lady in a man's skin. To such an extent is their feeling that they chose to undergo extensive surgery in order to have their male 'parts' removed and replaced with female 'parts'. This obviously shows how strongly they feel about their desires, their feelings and it must be 'more that I want to', it's a must for them to have this change and become as close as possible to a female as man's capability in the medical world will permit. Obviously the creation of children is not possible as only a born female can achieve this wonderful creation.

When you ask yourself, "what made this person feel so strongly that they wanted to undergo such surgery?" it's obvious that something inside them delivers a message that becomes so compelling, there is no alternative other than to purse surgery as life as a man, just becomes intolerable. Personally for this man, I admire their courage as this is not something that you can just try and, like and outfit, if it's not right, return it. No far from that, it's a one way street and there is now return. Once a man has made this choice, he lives with it for the rest of his life.

Reading articles on the subject and having certain feelings myself which obviously result in me wanting to dress in ladies clothes from time to time, it must come as a huge relief whereby they finally, can relax and purse being a full time female, a woman of their creation and live their lives in some form of more contentment than before. The acceptance of such a person seems to be more tolerated today and, I feel this is a good thing as why should anyone chose to persecute such a man who has this continuous feeling and actually lives every day as a huge burden being a man or, trying to be one?

There are many facets to this subject and I'm far from qualified or an expert on the subject, however I do understand and sympathize with these men who have this genuine desire and make the 'change'. There are others who for whatever reason feel they'd just like to experience the female aspect of sex and have yet another full filment of their sexual desire as the 'usual type of sex' doesn't bring to them the satisfaction they are looking for. They enter into sex with other men and obviously wish to play the part of the female and, beg to have their body so reconstructed in order that they can play this part and, enjoy this experience. It may be to full fill their partners, desire or their own, which ever it's related to some form of sexual activities and for this, they

43

purse to have surgery. For me, I feel this is somehow false and don't support their desires. It's a person choice and, I suppose because I am a man who has no desires or feelings toward other men of a sexual nature and, am only attracted to women, then like many other men, it's the way we are and, the most normal of all. Men are attracted to women, women are attracted to men. For all intents and purposes, man and woman were made to live together and reproduce similar to any animal on this planet, it's a give natural right.

There are men who obviously have the desire to live with and, enter into sexual relationships with other men and for this, it's their choice and as stated in earlier chapters, I'm not writing this book to state what is right or wrong on this subject. When men chose to abuse their privileges in life and enter into 'wrong doings' then for certain I condemn every aspect of this and, have zero tolerance for such behaviours.

In trying to understand if childhood influences have any bearing on the desire for a boy, teenager or man to want to dress in ladies clothes, I personally believe that influences from the time when a man was just a mere baby developing in his mother's womb, at that time certain 'things' could have influences and, after being bore in the early growing stages. Perhaps I'm entirely wrong and will let you and others who are better qualified to make judgment.

If a woman who wanting a child and, wants a baby girl feels so strongly in her mind about this, then perhaps those feelings are made known through whatever way to her baby and, this could result in at that early stage of development, cause for the baby to have that 'touch of female' desire even then. May be this is nonsense, for you and other's to decide, however I feel it has such a bearing and perhaps plants the seed of the desire. Please understand under no circumstances do I believe this is a woman's fault, far from it as actually while modern technology exists and you can now

44

understand the sex of a baby before it's born, I prefer not to know until it actually arrives. This is me and perhaps an old fashioned approach, however it's the approach my wife and I have chosen over the years [scanning was done back then].

Those desires and thoughts of a woman, who perhaps so desperately wants a baby girl, could be transferred to her baby. This 'could be one aspect of why a man has these desires to dress in ladies clothes the other, is during his younger years before becoming a teenager.

We are all influenced by what we see, what we taste and what we feel. It's human nature and brings our inquisitive mind and nature which has caused the human race of this world to prosper. Prosper and develop though not always for the better as man has made some serious blunders and, continues to do so. Wars, fighting, racial conflicts and ethnic believes have created huge rifts between nations of this world and sad to say, will continue for the duration of life on this planet. Evil for whatever reason is the cancer of life and until today, there is no sure onetime fix. Jealousy brings about much of these totally illogical and avoidable disasters, and we are all victims of "such wrong doings".

Given that what we see brings our minds to think and wonder is a gift and, enables us to all explore every facet regardless of large or small our curiosity takes us. If we are attracted to the aroma of a food, then this brings about our desire to want to taste it and from there, we make the choice if we like it or not. Take for instance the smell / aroma of bacon cooking on a cold morning when you're out walking. It just drifts across! It's a smell for many that brings instant hunger and the desire for a bacon sandwich with your favourite sauce and may be, a mug to tea. For others who chose the vegetarian way of life, they find the smell perhaps repulsive and it actually turns them off the thought of food.

These are personal choices and all influenced by what we see and feel at some time or other.

My childhood up bringing was idyllic to say the least. I had two wonderful parents, uncles and aunties, a big brother and friends and neighbours and was never subjected to any abuse or mistreatment either at home, school or in my leisure time. We lived as 'normal a life' as I would imagine and in a part of the world that had countryside, coast and hills, rivers and streams. Combined them all together and for certain, it brings an ideal up bringing for a child and, I have always felt this as a privilege and so much so, that my wife had a similar upbringing and we have provided the same for our children. It's something we value so much and we both aspire to and really enjoy the 'basic simple things in life'.

Attending school and making friends all brought new experiences for me and something I enjoyed though, school itself wasn't somewhere I really liked going to as there was so many other wonderful things in life to explore and do! Before going to school, and not long after I was born, my mother was taken ill with a life threatening condition, TB or more commonly known as Tuberculosis. Given that she was placed in hospital for many months, in fact over a year, I was brought up then by my grandmother who was a wonderful lady someone I liked so much. Obviously, she fed and looked after men and for this while I never knew at the time, I'm very grateful for however, perhaps her influences on my brought about may be, and I say may be just a hint of me being treated as a little girl for a while. If I can explain, apparently I was born with a good head of hair and this grew to be curly and very attractive. It wasn't cut for quite some time and there photos of me and you'd think at first glance I was a little girl. The many stories I've heard of how I, had such lovely long curly hair which everyone liked and, made me look like a girl, could this have somehow added to the influences of my desire for ladies clothes? It's a question and brings me to wonder.

Later, as my mother was release from hospital after making a good recovery, she had to attend hospital checkups on a regular base in order to ensure her condition was cured and no signs of re-occurrence. The nearest hospital was in the next major town which was an hour's bus ride away and she would attend them on what seemed a three monthly / quarterly bases. She would take me with her and I really enjoyed this as it meant a ride upstairs of a double decker bus! Going up stairs was something special as we would use down stairs for shorter trips and, being on the upper deck you could see so much more, it was just wonderful and, I'd really look forward to such outings. Perhaps my mother didn't view them like me, however in understanding that she made a good recovery and it's never returned, she's obviously gained satisfaction from the whole recovery ordeal over the years.

On one such outing, for whatever reason, the lady who used to live next door to us also came along and I was put to stay with her who was visiting a friend in the same town. For me this didn't make any difference as it meant a ride of the upper deck of the bus. The route took us along the coast and you could see the sea and I very much liked the seaside and all it brought with it.

This particular day, it was raining and we walked down to the bus stop and waited for the bus to arrive. Sure enough when it pulled up and we climbed on board and took a seat up stairs with me perched by the window. It was damp and wet but never the less; the excitement of the ride didn't dampen joy of this wonderful long ride as perceived it to be then. The bus passed the hospital which was on the sea front and, my mother got off here saying as soon as she was done with her checkup, she'd come to our neighbours flat. We arrived at

47

the town bus station and fortunately this flat was above a shop in a street just behind the bus station which only meant a short walk. I was quite happy and liked our neighbour, she was a fun sort of person and somehow I was comfortable in her company. We walked through the back alley of the bus station across the street the apartment door and after ringing the bell; the lady answered and invited us both in out of the rain. I'd never been in an apartment before as we lived in a bungalow with everything on the ground floor including a drive, gardens and a garage. It was somehow strange but interesting and when we climbed the stairs from the small front door, much to my surprise it opened up to a sort of normal house 'upstairs' so to speak. It was different but never the less felt cozy and they soon made me feel welcome.

The lady who owned the apartment also owned a stationery shop below, so obviously this was convenient for her work. Looking through the window in the front room, this was exciting as it looked out directly over the street and being as it was at the back of the bus station, all of the buses coming to town would pass this window! With other traffic it was good looking out as our front room window at home only opened out on to the garden, however something told me I preferred our house to this one if only to have the outside freedom as here, you could only step outside onto the street.

The lady gave me some pencils and paper to use for drawing, however I used them to take down car registration numbers and the numbers of all of the buses that passed. It was really good fun and kept me more than busy. Another lady arrived at the flat and obviously with three ladies now talking, this didn't' interest me at all and I continued to focus on 'car spotting' as this was much more fun. The third lady came over to say hello, again very nice and I shook her hand, and then continued with my new found hobby!

It must have been about half an hour later when the traffic eased that I'd time to look around at the flat and all of its content. The ladies had gone through to another room and I could hear them talking, then one came through in a dressing gown and as clear as day, I can remember her saying "are you alright dear?" for which I replied "yes thank you". I went back over to the window and the traffic was back so I was busy again jotting down as many numbers as I could. Hear the ladies again, our neighbour had come back into the room and was wearing just her underwear and even at that age it sort of shocked me a little as I'd never been exposed to this sort of lay behaviour before. She too asked me I was alright and I answered the same when the lady who owned the apartment appeared also in her underwear. They seemed to be trying on clothes, perhaps they had bought some new ones to try and were giving each other a go to see if they liked them. All three of them appeared which I found sort of strange at that age, one in a dressing gown and two in their underwear and they made their way to the kitchen which was sort of open to the front room. They made some tea and one of them brought me a glass of orange and some biscuits. She was still only wearing her underwear and being sort of embarrassed, I continued to look out of the window. However, she asked me how many numbers I'd managed to take down so I showed her my list. She came very close and I can remember even at that age, she didn't seem to mind standing in front of me with not many clothes on.

From what I can remember she was wearing some sort of girdle or body shaper as they are known today and stockings, nothing else. It was an embarrassing experience but somehow, I found that looking at her as she walked back to the kitchen very interesting. After they had made tea or coffee, they all came over to me too make admiring noises to this little boy who was car spotting and said what a long list

I'd made and generally talked to be about cars and buses. Again, even at that age I found their clothes very interesting. One of them [and I can't remember which one] was wearing pink underwear with tan stockings and, a pair of high heels!

I often thought about that experience many times over the years and wondered why they chose to only wear their underwear in front of me and walk around the place like that. Certainly they never did me any harm and I've no reason to believe that their reasoning was to perhaps try on some clothes, may be wedding outfits or some other special occasion outfit? Who would know? This was in reality my first exposure to ladies underwear and it somehow stayed with me for many years, in fact until today and that would have been some fifty three years ago.

Later my Mum arrived back after her hospital visit and by this time the ladies where dressed. She came over to me and I showed her my car spotting list and she commented on the amount of numbers I'd managed to collect. They all had a drink of tea and my Mum was busy talking to them for a while and I carried on spotting, then later that afternoon is was time for us to return home. We put on our coats and said good byes then made our way to the bus station and, I was first to get up stairs and take my place by the window making sure I was on the opposite side to when I came in the morning so I could still see the seaside and the railway line which ran across the golf course. It was again a fun ride home and that evening, I can remember mentioning to my Mum about the ladies only wearing their 'undies'. She didn't seem to make much of it and it was never mentioned again. Never mentioned again, however I thought about it many times. In fact their clothes, under clothes that is really intrigued me and, until this day has provided the same fascination.

That was an experience that I believe had some sort of influence on me and has seemed to have added to my fascination. I probably saw my Mum at some point dressing, though I can't ever remember any particular occasion and nothing ever stuck in my mind of this subject. As I've explained, looking at the catalogues in the coining years when playing with my train set and lying on the floor, I somehow connected the experience of seeing those ladies dressed as they were. It was some years later when I had another experience which again, stayed with me for many years and I believe kept and even enhanced my interests and desires.

At the age of eleven to twelve, I was working as a part time job on the farm and learning all of the skills involved with milking and looking after animals which I really enjoyed. Every aspect of farming I found interesting from the machinery to feeding calves, from mucking out to building hay barns and whatever else came along. I'd also started another job delivering milk on a Friday evening and Saturday with a great guy who I became friends with and have remained in touch even until today and he and his wife run a shop and market stall.

Meeting more and more people seemed somehow part of growing up and I really enjoyed this as many of our neighbours and people living local to us must have seen me growing up. My Mum was still working in the local corner shop and many people used to ask her if I'd do some small jobs for them like clearing rubbish from their gardens or helping to clean out their garages. It was good fun and I enjoyed it as it was more pocket money for savings and, sometimes they would give you items that they were disposing of! This included a whole host of interesting things from wind up gramophones and records to furniture and all sort of what I thought of as "good stuff" though, perhaps my

Mum and Dad had different ideas when I'd arrive home with arms full of junk!

One lady who lived just at the end of our road had a nice bungalow which was situated on a back and over looked the junction and, on my way home from school one afternoon I found my Mum was talking to her. They were both standing by the drive way gates. She was a very attractive lady, always looked somehow smart and well dressed, one of those ladies who always wore make up and had her hair done and earrings, well that's the way I remember her. Not so long back I was talking to my Mum about her as she came up in conversation and, my Mum said exactly the same. Perhaps this and other experiences that I've explained planted the intrigue in me, and made me curious as to why, did ladies wear such different clothes, interesting clothes, clothes that as I grew year by year became more fascinating for me.

After the usual conversation of asking how I was doing and how was school, my Mum said that this lady was wondering if I'd give her a hand in the garden as she had lots of shrubs that needed thinning out and the old branches and leaves would need taking away. I was only too pleased to help as it meant a bit more pocket money and this always came in handy. She was a nice lady who always said hello and it was good to think I was going to help her as her husband worked away, overseas in some hot location through I can't exactly remember where!

We set a date for a Saturday morning and I arrived as planned at 9:00. She was the sort of lady who even if she was working in the garden, she dressed for the occasion and always looked smart. Knocking at the back door she answered and said she's be with me in a few minutes so I parked my bicycle and waited by the garage door. She joined me and we opened up the garage to find everything in place perfectly, it was a real pleasure just to see! We picked out the tools we needed and set to cutting back some branches that were leaning from the hedge of the bungalow next door. It had over grown badly and looked rather a mess in comparison with her well-manicured lawns and flower beds. I did most of the cutting and we bundled up the branches into rolls that I could then carry on my bike to the local rubbish tip. While she brushed up, I took for the first load then the second, strapping the bundles to my crossbar. It was a bit difficult to peddle, however it didn't really matter as all but for a small brow, it was all downhill on the way there.

As the morning went on she made some tea and brought it for us both, we worked well together, and it was actually good fun, then at lunch time we stopped and said we'd carry on next Saturday when I would be off school again. Sure enough, the next Saturday came around and we continued with our clearing which was going well. I needed to use the toilet and said I'd nip home for which she replied, "nonsense, go in the house and use ours". I took off my boots and carefully followed her to the bathroom door and then went in and shut the door behind me. To say the least it was a beautiful room, very stylish and well decorated and, I proceeded with my business! The loo was situated in sort of a small alcove and directly opposite was a towel rail which was loaded with neatly pressed and folded clothes she'd put to air. Indeed, mostly they were ladies under clothes of all types. One of them I clearly remember was a suspender belt in sort of a pale pink colour with metal clasps, some black stockings and satin knickers all there on display in front of me! I didn't have much time as my 'business' was soon done and I then washed my hands and left the room. She was in the kitchen making a drink and I called through thanking her for the use of her loo. "No problem, your welcome any time" was her reply as she carried the two mugs of tea outside.

That evening as was the norm for a Saturday evening, I watched TV with my mother as Dad was away working and my brother was stopping over at a friend's house. I'm not sure what was on the TV and to be honest was not really interested and the only thing on my mind was this ladies underwear. They looked expensive and good high quality as she was the sort of lady who bought good things and, the house was immaculate. In the coming weeks and months I regularly gave her a hand in the garden though never did I need to use her bathroom, though the thought of her underwear drying / airing on that towel rail stayed with me for many years!

I think I should explain here that my feelings toward her clothes where purely with my inquisitive mind for trying them on, or at least wanting to try on similar when the time would eventually come for me. She was a nice lady, if that word nice sums her up as she was both kind and courteous and would always make a point of stopping to talk. She would always have time for me and my Mum who was quite friendly with her and, for some years to come I was her 'part time' gardener. Often in the summer when they would go off on vacation, I would trim the lawns and edges making sure that everything where right for their return. Somehow, while she paid me well, it was just a pleasure to help her; she was just a good person.

Over these last few paragraphs, I've tried to illustrate that perhaps, and I can only say perhaps, my childhood upbringing and, my early teenage years had some influence on my desire to dress in ladies clothes. I must also state here that, my only desire was to wear ladies underwear, stockings, suspenders, bras, knickers, girdles and all of those foundation garments I'd looked at over the years in those home shopping catalogues. As for any desire to perhaps have any affair with a lady, this never entered my

54

head. My desire was purely with the clothes. After leaving school and starting work taking on a new life, only then did I begin to see the attraction of ladies and like most young men, had a few girl friends on and off and enjoyed the social life that it brought. During these years for whatever reason my desire to dress remained with me, however it somehow took on a back seat in my mind and never really flushed again until after I was married.

Could these childhood years when others thought I was a girl through having long curly hair had any influence on me? Could that time when I stayed with those ladies in the flat added to those influences and, in later years given these desires never left me where brought back out to the for front of my mind when I noticed those clothes airing on the towel rail? These questions I've asked myself time and time again and never concluded an answer.

Perhaps by now you're thinking I'm some sort of weirdo, and I don't really blame you as we're all entitled to our opinions. Even today, right now as I type this sentence and asking the question "would I like to dress right now" the answer is yes! Those feelings are as strong as ever and I'm happy with them. Happy in knowing I can put on some of my favourite clothes and enjoy the feel, the sensation of the materials on my skin, the looks in the mirror and the feeling of enjoyment. Nothing has changed fifty something years on. Do I feel ashamed of this in any way? No, I'm pleased that I have these feelings and, knowing that I can control them and enjoy life. Does it really do any harm to anyone, the answer is no, providing that others in your life are respected, that is their thoughts and opinions are taken into consideration. What do you think? Was there some influence that added to my desires during my early years? I can't right now think of any others, however during the writing of this book if any come to mind, I'll revert back.

Chapter 7

Dressing in my man clothes

Clothes are important to everyone and we should all take a certain amount of pride in our appearance. I certainly like to look the part for every occasion whether is just pottering round the garden, shopping for groceries or visiting friends, I like to look that part. I'm not a man who could be termed as a snappy dresser, in fact quite the opposite as I like more traditional clothes and believe clothes can serve for many years if looked after.

Every so often, I'll have clear out and load up the bags for a trip to the charity shops as for certain, clothes bought sometimes for an occasion become dated and you no longer see yourself using them. For instance, you can buy a few tee shirts when on holiday and they look fine at the time and, many be for the odd bbq at home, however the next time you look at them your mind has changed completely and you feel they are no longer suit your tastes. Those sort of casual clothes are cheap enough that you can afford to change them as often as you like. I'll wear some outrageous coloured long shorts and a baggy shirt to do the garden, however if I've a reason to go to the shop perhaps for a paper or come other incidental, then I'll change into some more suitable clothes and on my return, change again back into those gardening clothes.

We all have different tastes and many men find socks for instance really boring, however I delight when someone buys me some good socks be they, long thick green wooly ones for walking in the winter months or, some nice socks for everyday and work. My favourite of all socks are long stretchy ones that you can pull up and that stay up. It's so frustrating when they immediately wriggle their way down your legs and end up in a heap around your ankles. These type of socks are destined only for one of two places, back to the shop from which they were purchased or, the bin! Many people find taking clothes back that don't fit or perform as they should as a real challenge. This shouldn't be so as the manufacturer if half decent, usually likes feedback in order to rectify any problems. If you don't take things back and let them know, they can't do anything about it. If you've no idea where they came from if perhaps received as a present, then bin here they come.

Pulling on socks is something I very much enjoy, in fact I always have and right up until today making sure you're toes are in the correct place with the seam across the front on line and then putting your heel in the pocket is something to be enjoyed and makes for a comfortable wear to them. It's exactly the same when I put on a pair of stockings, they have to be rolled between your thumb and fingers in order that you can put your toes in the right place and ensure the seam in correct across them, then roll the stocking over your foot and make sure the heel is nicely fitting and, if you're putting on seams, then as you roll and pull them up your leg make sure they are not twisted. Putting on socks or putting on stockings both have their own pleasures, however the end results are different and it depends on the occasion for which you're dressing. The feel of wooly socks for instance is brilliant inside some good walking boots or wellingtons and, it's lovely to have your feet all snug and warm. That being said it's wonderful to put on a pair of new stockings and feel the nylon of silk move against your skin as you walk to the mirror to admire yourself, purely magic! Bending over to straighten a seam and looking at your legs clad with some nice tan or black stockings really is a sensation unequalled compared with wearing any men's clothes!

Most of my clothes are bought from M&S and even from an early age I can remember the labels having St. Michael's on them which used to be the M&S brand name. For underwear I like white colour and proper underpants that give you the necessary support you need. How men can wear boxer shorts is beyond me as something's need to be held in place! Underwear that clings and hugs my body with high waste bands really appeal to me as somehow they feel like wearing a pull on panty girdle or, some other type of ladies shape wear. I'm not a fan of panty girdles simply because you have limited access to those necessary parts when it comes to the loo and, wearing knickers under them is something I find quite uncomfortable.

Yes, as you'll have gathered, being comfortable is something I really must be when dressed even if I'm wearing a pair of overalls to work on the car, it has to fit right and not be to tight or by stark contrast, a silky blouse, it can't be too tight either or to wear one that ruckles up and looks as though it doesn't fit right!

My feelings toward wearing both ladies and gents clothes are the same it's just that they are for a different occasion and bring different feelings and levels of comfort.

For work, my clothes are quite straight forward, smart casual trousers and white shirts with a tie of needed. Many men complain that they have to wear a tie, for me it's no more that wearing any other piece of clothing and doesn't bother if I've to wear one all day or not, depending on the circumstances. I've a large selection of ties bought from all over the world and again, depending on the occasion I'll chose what I believe to the most fitting for the day. I'm quite particular about the knot and like to have a well-balanced half Windsor type. Just tying a tie as though it's a piece of string doesn't do it for me at all and even though in some circles it can be seem as hip and trendy, not for good old fashioned me !

As for jackets, again worn to suit the occasion be it walking over the hills all wrapped up in a Barbour jackets and cap with matching scarf and gloves or, a long water proof rain coat and wellington boots. There is nothing nicer that being dressed for whatever the weather is going to throw at you and know, you're dry and comfortable underneath. My selection of jackets is varied from smart dinner suit type through to waxed jackets and casual for the occasions.

Probably at this point you're thinking how boring this guy is! I'd like to point out that I am in every sense of the word a normal sort of guy with normal traditional dressing habits and, this is how I have and always will dress. Do I want to wear some silk knickers under my man clothes? No! Definitely not, as there is a time and a place for those sort of clothes. Can you imagine what it would be like if for any reason you were rushed to hospital and had to have your clothes removed? The nurses would have a hay day taking off your clothes and the embracement would be something I'd rather not think about! Similarly, wearing stockings and a suspender belt under my work clothes, no not for me not least because, stocking rubbing up against trousers are not a very nice feeling and, what would be the point? Yes certainly I like to dress in ladies clothes, however there is a time and place to relax and enjoy. Perhaps and I am sure there are men who don't get the opportunity to wear ladies clothes in their home environment and, for that reason will wear them at work being careful to put them on at the right time and, remember to take them off before going home. It's quite sad in a way that, a fully grown man who has all of the responsibilities of the world on his shoulders and yet, he can't wear a pair of knickers in his own house. The fear of being found out, someone knowing of your liking and fondness toward ladies underwear, or may be a little make up and some high heels. It's quite absurd really when you think about the whole subject yet, the true reality is if you have this desire and people get to know about it, you're immediately branded as someone with strange and 'out of the norm' habits. Someone who could be looking at all sorts of undesirable photos on the web, someone who could have other sexual desires and, someone who could be cheating on his wife or partner! You immediately become branded and, if the media finds out, then it's a chance to sell newspapers so they would have a hay day.

So before dressing in ladies clothes underneath your normal man's type clothing, it really needs to careful thought as the quite innocence of desires could become a complex situation that could affect your whole life to come.

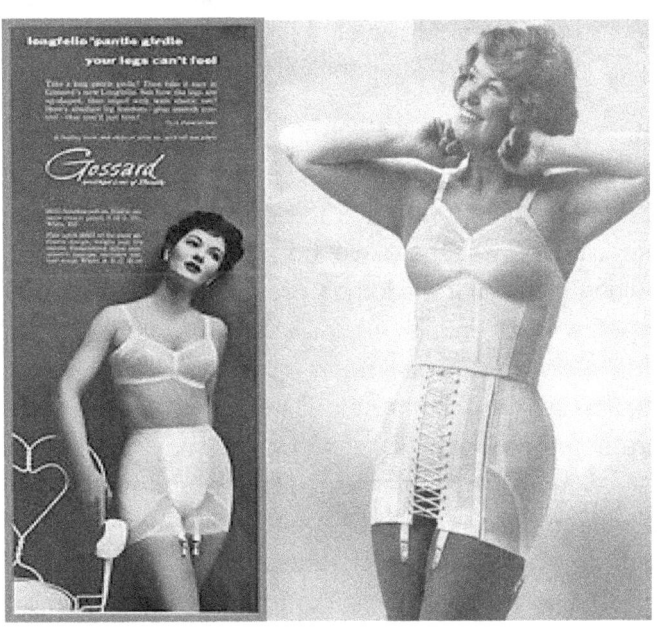

Chapter 8

Dressing in my ladies clothes

Writing about my dressing in ladies clothes is something I really feel, it's important for me to provide an explanation for those who wonder 'why?' It's the main reason for me writing this book in order to share everything possible in order to for you to try and draw a conclusion in your mind.

Is this book going to provide 'the answer', somehow I doubt it! It will bring some light on the subject and for certain, let others who have the same desires and, for those who perhaps are wondering if they should or, shouldn't try on some clothes provide them with an insight of what it entails. Equally, for those loved ones, partners, wives who really question what's the attraction and are wondering if they should / shouldn't tolerate such behavior for their man, it may bring some relief of more understanding. Please understand I'm not writing this as a book to "try and convince" or persuade anyone that men dressing in ladies clothes from time to time is 'normal' and that there's nothing wrong with it. Far from it! That is for you to determine and it will bring another explanation for this desire and add to the already known stories, explanations and facts which may trigger the professionals who are qualified to analyses such desires and for those people to bring us all a little closer to the understanding of 'what makes men want to dress in ladies clothes?'

Dressing up in ladies clothes is a desire I have from time to time and, if not in the mood and don't have the feelings, then I've no interest to think any further. Similarly, writing about dressing in ladies clothes takes on two perspectives. If I feel the desire, then writing about the sensation, the experience, the desire, is easy. However if I don't have those feelings, it's not easy to explain   and truthfully, just about as boring a subject that I could think to try and write about. Right now as I type this paragraph, am I interested and want to dress in those clothes? No! It's just about the furthest thing away in the back of my mind. You'll probably find this difficult to believe, however it's true. I'll break now and continue when my feelings come on and I want to dress and, I'll use *italic font* in order that you know when I'm in that mood and can best describe exactly what those feelings are toward wearing my ladies clothes.

From that early age, I've mainly had a fascination for ladies underwear and chose to experiment with a hook & eye side fastening white open bottom girdle and some tan nylon stockings. The feeling when I first put them on was just delightful and, right now I have that very feeling! I'm going to describe exactly what has happened today and how my feelings arrived. Also, I'll share the clothes I'm going to change into and keep writing about my feelings.

It's been an ordinary sort of day with nothing new to report, this means I've been to work and had a good day achieving what I set out to achieve and came home to my wife preparing our evening meal. It's still winter time so it's been a cold but dry day and there's nothing better than coming into a nice warm cozy home. I use the term home as that's what we prefer to think of our house, it's our home. After the usual chit chat and a shower, then sitting down to a nice meal, I asked if we were going anywhere this particular evening in order to know if I could put the car away or leave it out. We'd nowhere in mind to go to so I put the car in and we settled down by the TV for the evening. Not really taking any interest in the TV, I was reading the paper and suddenly thought, "It would be nice to change into some evening clothes, some underwear and a dressing gown". I asked my wife if she'd mind if I went and got changed and she said not at all, so long as I brought her a cup of tea!

The house was all warm and all of the curtains drawn. I popped through to the kitchen and filled the kettle and got out a few mugs and the tea pot. One the kettle had boiled; I filled the tea pot in order for it to brew properly. I went upstairs and had a look in my underwear draw and looked through my selection of stockings, girdles, bras and suspender belts. Whatever the reason, I chose black as my colour for the evening and picked out some nice seamed stockings. I've several pairs and the one's I'd chosen had a 'Cuban' type heel and lovely

64

seams that go the full length of the stocking right the way up to the top. I draped them over the nice white bed linen and admire them for a while and then decided I'd wear a suspender belt. I've several to choose from, however only two are in black colour so, I chose one that seems to be my favourite which has eight suspender straps and four hook & eye fastenings at the back. It's also got a pretty bow in the middle of the front waist line and, is made of a lovely stretchy type plain fabric which really hugs to my waist and tummy. I draped this next to my stockings and pondered if I should wear a waspie, girdle or should I have a treat and wear my lace up corset? I've only on in black colour and couldn't quite make my mind up.

As usual, choosing what to wear is all part of the fun and warm feeling that my dressing desire brings, however the tea would be well brewed by now so, I returned down stairs and poured our tea. Taking to the front room, my wife was engrossed in an evening 'soap' and hardly moved her eyes from the TV muttering a 'thank you'

I returned upstairs with my mug of tea and then looked at what I'd chosen. Perfect and, I decided to wear my lace up corset and my midi bra. Picking out my corset, I laid it on the bed and made sure the lace's where undone properly. There's a knack to putting on and taking off a corset, I'll share this with you later! My feelings are just true excitement and I can't wait to put my clothes on!

It's a personal choice, however choosing the right bra is important as it like all other clothes as to fit properly and be comfortable to wear and, look good! Draping my bra over the bed, I looked at my chosen outfit and agreed, yes these are what I want to wear and I'm sure I'll feel good in them!

Taking off my usual evening 'around the house' clothes and putting them away, I picked up my suspender belt and put it on. With practice, fastening it behind my back is easy and placing the hooks in the eyes is something I really like doing. Once it was around my waist, I turned to the mirror to check that it was straight and that the suspenders where undone to the maximum length as I like to adjust each one in turn to ensure I've got the right tension of my stockings. It looked just right and felt to say the least just wonderful and I must have spent five minutes or more just admiring myself wearing only my suspender belt.

There are many different types of suspender belts and, most of the ones you see in the high street shops are truly rubbish in my opinion! They must be designed for someone how has no feeling for comfort and, has no understanding of wearing stockings! They are usually very narrow around the waist and, have only four suspender straps which are useless to hold your stockings in place. Stockings need to be well supported and this means having a minimum of eight straps to hold them up, anything less and you'll find them slipping and feeling uncomfortable. Remember, if you're wearing stockings, they need to look good and feel good regardless what you're doing or, where ever you plan to go. Needless to say, your suspender belt *needs to be comfortable and provide the correct support for your stockings, they work together!*

Once I'd finished admiring myself and doing the odd 'twirl' and seeing my suspender straps flying out then falling back on my legs, [a wonderful feeling I must add and, something you need to experience if you're contemplating wearing stockings and suspenders] I picked up my stockings and went and sat down on our dressing table stool.

Stocking are wonderful! The feel and look are something that again gives me a very warm and comfortable feeling and I can't wait to put them on. You learn by doing as they same and a piece of advice, make sure you have either short nails, or nails that are well manicured and have no sharp bits sticking out as these can catch on your stockings. Not only is the feeling of changing a sharp nail on your stockings something that's not nice, chances are you will put a hole or make a ladder in them. Once you've done this, I'm afraid the only answer is to put them in the bin. When you first start dressing, you always make these mistakes, however the thrill and fulfillment of your desire over rides the fact that you've just wasted several pounds on a pair of stocking that you've not even had chance to look when you're dressed! So, make sure your nails have no sharp nicks or rough parts, this is speaking from experience!

Taking one at a time and usually my left side first, I roll the stocking between my thumb and fore fingers using both hands until it's neatly bunched up and my fingers are in the toe section. Then carefully, I place the stocking over my toes and make sure that the seam across the toes is straight from one side to the other. Once I'm quite happy, I'll pull the stocking over my heel and check to see that the heel is straight and that the seam is in the centre. Again, if everything looks good then I'll roll out my stocking pulling it gentle up to my knee, then I'll usually stand up. It helps to stand as it's not easy to pull a stocking around a bent knee. Pulling my stocking up my leg is something I really enjoy and making sure that seam is straight all the way up the back. This usually means a quick look in the mirror. Once I'm sure my stocking seam is straight and that it feels comfortable, I'll attached the first suspender strap and, usually I'll chose the one that dangles straight down in the front of my leg. It's important not to move too much and walk around as if you do, then your stocking will wriggle a little and move down which usually ends up with a wrinkled knee – Norah Batty style!!

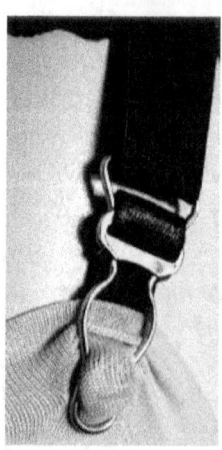

Fastening my suspender, I put one finger behind the button and put this under my stocking top then, using my other hand, carefully place the eye of the suspender on the outside and press the button through my stocking top and push the eye of the button, then pull eye up over the button. This grips my stocking and holds it firmly in place! It's important when you chose a suspender belt to make sure all the fastening are metal ones and not plastic. Plastics ones stretch and come undone and, there's nothing more annoying than a suspender that comes undone and you find your stocking coming down your leg!

After making sure my first suspenders is in place, I'll then fasten the back one which is not so easy but, with a little practice it soon becomes second nature and all part of the fun of dressing! It takes a few goes to get this one right as it's important to have the stocking seam gripped by the suspender as this will hold it taught in place and when you stand up straight, it's pull and hold it exactly where you want it to be. Again, placing one finger under the bottom, I'll place this under my stocking top and feel for the seam. Remember, you're doing this bent over and behind your back and the mirror usually comes in handy to see if it's in the right place. Once there, using my other hand I'll slip over the eye on the outside of my stocking top until I can feel it over the button, then I'll slide up and it's done. Next I'll fasten the suspender that's dangling on the outside of my leg using the same method and, making sure it's straight with my leg and not pulling to the back or front. Lastly I'll fasten the final one that's on the inside of my leg again going through the same wonderful process.

Now that I've one stocking in place, time for a glance in the mirror and I'm happy with what I see and the feeling is just wonderful. I look at the back, the heel, the seam and my stocking top admiring what I see. Going back to the stool, I put on my right stocking going through the same careful process and enjoying the absolutely wonderful sensation and feeling it brings to me. Putting on stockings is really a pleasure to experience and something I enjoy so much.

After making sure they are all fastened properly, I stood up and adjusted the tension on the straps starting with the front and then the rear one. After making sure these are good – just enough tension, I adjusted the outside and inside ones. Once done, I turned to the mirror to admire the view – just wonderful! Wow! Just look at me, wearing my black seamed stocking held up with my eight strap suspender belt! I've walked up and down in front of the mirror admiring myself just wearing stockings and my favourite belt. They feel wonderful, the nylons stockings next to my legs and the stretchy material of my suspender belt around my waist feels so supportive with my straps adjusted and my seams straight up the back of my legs.

Now it's time for my knickers, I'd actually forgotten to pick these out of my undies draw purely because of excitement! Looking through my selection, I chose a pair with a narrow back strap that sits comfortably in my bottom and they have a good wide front and waist band. The elastic in these is firm but not tight and they are amazingly comfortable to wear. The front panel has some lace and a ribbon bow in the middle and, the elastic around the legs at the front is again firm and this is important in order to hold my manly parts in place! Pulling on pair of knickers is again a wonderful feeling! I stood in front of the mirror and bent over lifting my left leg and carefully put my stocking clad toes and foot through the hole and pulling it up my leg slightly, and then I did the same with my other foot. The feeling of nice soft silky / satin knickers up against stocking clad legs is no less that pure bliss! I pulled them up over my knees and then carefully side at a time, pulling them up over my suspenders taking care not to catch them on the metal clips. Once up I straightened them and had another glance in the mirror, wow do they look good and feel just wonderful. There is very something special about having your manly parts held nice and firm in silk or satin, you can only really understand the experience by wearing a pair.

Feeling all well supported, that is firmly held together feeling in my favourite underwear is something special, they feel good and look good and if I say it myself, I look good in the mirror too! The bra I chose was again one of my favourite, a black full cup, 42DD with ten hook and eye fastenings at the rear with wide shoulder straps. Putting on a bra is something to be again experienced! It's important to have the right bra and, as always a comfortable one that fits you well and, look's good.

Choosing a bra is an individual choice as you need to decide what you wish to look like once dressed in it. Some men chose a smaller cup size, B or C, however I prefer a larger size and chose a DD cup. Obviously dressing myself I like to create the appearance of a lady with a fuller figure and large bust. Again its personal choice however let me explain the type of bra I chose and the reasons why. When you chose to have a larger bust, obviously your in-fills [whatever type you chose] need to be well supported and provide the right shape you're hoping to achieve. Bras come in all shapes sizes and colours. I like a full cup none padded type bra and good shoulder straps to provide good support and feel comfortable if worn for many hours. The bra will determine you bust shape and for me, the fuller figured lady wearing a full cup bra brings out that classic shape that I like to achieve. I've several other bras, long and normal but all are full cup styles. When I wear In-fills, I like to have them totally covered by my bra so that they don't show when I bend over or stretch upwards.

I picked my bra up off the bed and placed my arms through the shoulder strap and put them over my shoulders then pulled both ends together behind my back. The feeling is pure bliss and fastening the hooks and eyes behind my back again is similar to fastening a suspender belt, it just takes a little time and experience to perfect. I can say after all these years, I can fasten them in the dark and it's a wonderful feeling when you've hooked in that final hook, all firm and feeling my chest being supported with my favourite bra. I had a glance in the mirror to check my shoulder straps and both where straight and looked good.

Walking over to my underwear draws, I opened the second one which contains my in-fills. There are many different types and I'll talk a little about these later. Placing first the left one in my bra cup, I gently pulled open my bra just enough to slip in and place my in-fill. Making sure that is was in the right place in my bra cup, I lifted up the other and placed that in my right cup again straightening and making sure it was in the right place. I turned to the mirror to admire my bust and it looks perfect, right shape, right size and right feel! There is something special about making sure you bra shoulder straps are correctly adjusted in order to give you the support you need and that little bit of bounce as you walk. Looking at myself in the mirror, I feel very pleased, very happy and somehow, very excited to know I'm wearing my ladies underwear clothes. The feeling is warm, well supported, all fastened up and the black colour against my skin looks wonderful. Indeed there is nothing more satisfying that looking at the results of my choice of underwear and the colours, style and feeling.

Looking at the only garment left on the bed, my lace up corset, I decided this would finish off my dressing for the evening. If you've never experienced wearing a lace up, it's something you need to do in order to understand the results and the wonderful feeling it brings. I picked it and made sure the laces, where fully in the undone position as if they're not, it would be impossible for me to fasten it. Holding either end where the fastening hooks are I turned it to make sure the inside would be next to my body. On each panel, there are two steel plates, on has holes and the other has some buttons that stock out and these hold the corset together in your front and, they really are firm. I placed it around my back where the laces dangle on my bottom and then bring around the ends to meet under my bust. This type of corset is known as an under bust style with a medium length body and it fits snuggly under my bust and down as far as the top of my hips. Wrapping it around my back, I brought the both ends to meet and just clipped the top eye on the button. It's up to you which one you chose I always chose the top one and make sure the corset is in the right position under my bust. If you can imagine me with my midi full cup bra, the corset actually covers the lower body part of my bra and this I find useful as it leaves no gaps between my bra and corset. This is one of the reasons I lake to wear my midi bra with a lace up corset though not on every occasion.

Fastening the hooks over the buttons is good fun as somehow they all have to line up and be done together. With the top one fastened, I brought the others in line and fed the buttons through the holes and all of a sudden, it's done! I'm in my corset and it feels wonderful! Lacing up takes some practice and there are many good tips on 'U TUBE' that show you how to lace up your corset by yourself. I looked at myself on the mirror and I always at this stage look at the outline of my figure which is quite straight as look down both sides, turning to the right I looked at my back and front to see my bottom protruding nicely from under my corset and my tum, sticking out a little after a rather large evening meal! The laces at this point of dressing in my corset are short, so I put my hands behind my back and feel for both lace loops and swap the right for the left and left for right. The reason here is simple. If you can imagine, when you pull the laces, you need to pull them in the direction from which they are threaded through as not to cause them to bind. Putting the loops over my thumbs, I gave them both a good tug until my arms are fully stretched out and, the magic begins to happen!

Looking at the lace panel on my back, the laces start to bunch a little at the top and bottom as they are pulled from the centre, so I use one had to hold the lace ends at my front and the other to pull the loose lace tight and work from the top down to the middle and bottom up to the middle. Once I'd removed the slack, I gave both laces another tug and this time they really start to tighten my corset and my waist line begins to shrink rapidly! Going through the same again, I gave a final tug on both laces and hey presto! my waist is formed and looks stunning! You can tie the laces in a bow behind yourself, however and speaking from experience, I don't recommend this as if they end up in a knot [and this is easy to happen!] then you really struggle to undo that knot behind your back and it can take many minutes or even hours to fathom out how to undo it without cutting the laces. I bring both laces to the front and tie them in a nice bow neatly and lave both ends dangle over my tum. The feeling is wonderful and being all strapped up is really a lovely feeling knowing your body is well supported and any bulge is discreetly taken care of.

At this point as always, I looked in the mirror and feel really pleased at what I see – me! Stood there in stockings, suspender belt, bra and corset, it's a sensation that goes beyond works and the looks achieved are really sensational. After a few walk up and downs in front of the mirror, a few bend overs and twirls, I make my final adjustments, bra strap on one side and suspender clips and I'm ready to go!

Now, "should I wear anything else?" I asked myself. Some heels perhaps? No, not this evening as I only wanted to wear my underwear and return to watch some TV. I put on my dressing gown and slippers, tidied my draws and then went downstairs to join my wife in the front room. I must have taken an hour to choose my clothes and get dressed, it's something I enjoy and don't like to rush. Asking how she was doing, she turned and asked me if I'd like a cup of coffee? Yes I said, 'would you like me to make one? "No was her reply, I'll make this one" and she made her way to the kitchen. Making myself comfortable on the couch, the feeling of my underwear next to my skin is really sensational and, wearing only my dressing gown over the top is also a lovely feeling as it's mad of satin and slides gently over my stocking clad knees, again a feeling which is pure bliss! There's a little bit of cool air around my stocking tops which again has to be experience to be believed, it's a very exciting and enjoyable feeling. The feeling of your bare leg at the top of your stocking and from your knickers leg is really a lovely experience and again, something you can only feel if you wear these clothes.

I relaxed for the evening and felt wonderful knowing I was dressed in my underwear. As I move and my dressing gown opens a little, it's nice to see my knee appear and then my stocking top. I don't make display of myself and like to keep covered, however leaning over to pick up the TV controller, it's nice to look down the front of my dressing gown and see my bust which is quite prominent being a DD size. I wrapped my dressing gown around me again and put my feet up on the sofa, the feeling of being so well supported in a corset and bra, having stockings cladding my legs is just wonderful.

My wife at this point said she was going to have a read in a nice warm bath and made her way upstairs. I heard the water running and her getting ready for her soak. With nothing of real interest on the TV, I decided to switch off and make my way up stairs and check email in our office. It's a snug warm room and a great place to work from. Switching off the lights I called up to my wife and asked if she wanted anything, however she didn't hear me so I shut off the lights and made my way to the office. Climbing the stairs wearing stockings is a lovely experience as they somehow seem to slide a little over your legs and the sensation of nylons or silk stockings on your skin is just a wonderful experience to say the least!

We have an office type chair which is really comfortable and swivels around to make getting in out of the desk easy. Again, sitting on the chair wearing stockings and my dressing gown that keeps opening revealing my stocking tops and suspender clips is just wonderful. I looked at a few emails, there was nothing exciting in them so opened some of my favourite web pages to look for ladies underwear and clothes. How different it is sitting here looking at all of the thousands of beautiful clothes as compared with all of those years ago, lying on the floor looking at the catalogue which was good at the time but somehow seem a little dated compared with today's technology.

I'd been fancying a new suspender belt and had seen one on E Bay, then after wadding through the many pages of items for sale until I came across the very one I was looking for. It's got a deep waist, about 6" in the front and has a hook and eye fastening just to one side of the centre front and, has eight hooks and eyes. It has all of the other important things I look for, metal clips and metal adjusters as these are important. Again, if you're thinking of buying a suspender belt to wear, make sure you have metal clips as these are the best for keeping your stockings properly in place. Keeping the page, I marked it and continued to look at other items' I'd been fancying. Believe it or not, to buy a black, full cup midi or long bra in a 42 DD cups size is near impossible. You can buy white but, for whatever reason black seems to be out of fashionable favour right now. Anyway, I couldn't find anything else that took my fancy so, I just bought the suspender. I'll talk a little bit more about shopping later, its good fun and all part of the experience of dressing in ladies clothes.

I shut the light off in the office and went through to the bathroom to find my wife deeply engrossed in a good book. She's an avid reader and makes really good use of her Kindle and, she reads paper backs, in fact anything that takes her interest. I asked her if she'd had a good soak for which she replied yes and was going to top up the water with a little more warm. The bathroom was warm and I slipped off my dressing gown leaving me only in my under clothes. As she reached for the tap to turn on for some more hot water, she looked across at me over her glasses and said nothing, but somehow the quiet smile on her face told me a lot. I lay back in our easy chair and put my feet up admiring the view, my wonderful wife all relaxed in her bath and me, dressed in my lady clothes, what a wonderful evening it was.

After chatting for a while, she said she'd had enough so I picked a nice hot towel off the radiator and handed it to her as she stood up. Thanking me, I left her to dry herself off; meanwhile I went to our bedroom and had a final few glances of myself in the mirror, what a pleasing sight it was too! Always after getting dressed up, I take the same amount of care undressing, piece by piece and put them away all folded neatly in my underwear draws ready for next time. Firstly, I undid the laces for my corset and felt it relax slowly and open up, then with a little twist of my waist, it was full undone so I undid the front fastening clips and took it off. Folding clothes neatly is something I've learnt to do over the years and it makes a big difference when you come to wear them next time. I really like undoing my bra hooks and eyes at the back and then feeling the final one undone, I slip my bra off my shoulders leaning forward as my in-fills are still in place. Next I slide my knickers down to my ankles and one foot at a time, step out of them and picked them up off the floor placing them on the bed.

At this moment, my wife had come through from the bathroom and I was just starting to undo my stockings as she passed me and proceeded to get her sleeping pajamas out of her draws. I took my time undoing each suspender and then rolling each stocking off my legs and picking them up, off the floor. Totally undressed I put all my clothes away and dressed in my pajamas as well and pulled back the quilt to join her in bed. She was by this time; just on the point of nodding off and I thanked her for letting me dress that evening. She said 'you're welcome and was glad that I'd enjoyed myself and, her bath had made her feel really relaxed and sleepy'.

That is what I call a perfect evening, thinking what to wear, making sure my lovely wife is ok with me dressing and then picking out the clothes I've chosen and laying them on the bed. After that, getting undressed and starting to put on my clothes piece by piece is pure bliss and excitement! Each garment has its own feel, own material and own sensation both to look at and, when you put them close to your body. These sensations are all part of what of like about dressing and have done form that very early age.

Depending on my mood for dressing, I sometimes like to choose white underwear as this was the first colour I dressed in all those years ago and I do like white together with tan coloured stockings. I've worn tights from time to time but must say, I don't like them for the simple reason I feel so closed on with them if that makes sense. I can see that they are quite convenient in some ways as you don't need any suspenders to hold them up, but for me I much prefer stockings and that open feeling at the top of my legs and, the added convenience when going to the loo!

I've tried many types of stocking from cheap nylons to expensive silky ones and they all have their merit so to speak and, they have their place or the occasion. Sometimes, I like to wear just a suspender belt and some cheap, 'one size fits all' stockings in any colour. These are fund to wear for the occasion as they stretch and usually are not really long enough to come up high enough where I feel them to be comfortable on my legs. This means I have to lengthen the suspenders in order to attach them and it feels good seeing and knowing that they are pulling my stockings up my legs. The result is that my stocking tops are far from straight, in fact they are stretched up to reach my suspenders and have a feeling of tightness and undersize. They're only a bit of fun to wear and not practical for any other purpose and I usually end up taking them off and putting them straight in the bin. Again, it's what suits the mood and feeling at that particular time.

From time to time I like to wear girdles as these are something special for me and, have a unique feel to them as each one is different! I only have open bottom girdles in my collection as the panty girdles I find a bit of a challenge especially when I'm all dressed and need the loo! They are totally designed for ladies and there is no space for a man's 'parts' and make for an uncomfortable wearing session as everything is so to speak, 'squashed up' and quite annoying. I've two pull on girdles, one black and the other white and they provide good support to hold in my tum and provide a good shape to my bottom enhancing the outward bulges. The black on actually has a sort of cut out over the bottom which leaves my both cheeks exposed and these are somehow pushed down but the girdle and in so doing, are pushed out. Obviously wearing stockings with a girdle is a nice experience and the ones I have, are fitted with eight straps, however the strap lengths are not extendable and therefore pull on your stocking quite tightly. I actually like this feeling and as you can imagine, with those suspenders tugging on my stockings, the cut out top pushing down on my bottom upper cheeks, it makes my bottom stick out more than normal adding the 'lady like look' I like to achieve when dressing up. I'm quite fortunate that my body is regularly proportioned and with a little bit of effort it can soon take on a feminine shape, though I know for a fact it will never actually replicate the body of a true lady. All the same it's good fun trying and again, adds to the joy of dressing up.

My other girdles are hook and eye type fastening and are really a lot firmer than the pull on ones as they have bones running the full length to say them wrinkling up. One is a pink colour and I only like to wear this when my 'pink mood strikes' which is not very often. I bought secondhand and it was like new having had little wear. The other is black and actually has six suspender straps and while I usually insist on eight, the position of these straps is such that somehow it's comfortable to wear and gives my stocking the good support they need. Its fund dressing in them as the hook and eye fasteners on one are along the back panel, and on the other on the right hand side. I have to 'breathe in a little' when putting them on as there's not much give in them. Girdles are after all designed to provide support and that flattening effect for a ladies tummy and without having some rigidity, the effect is lost. Both have nice little bows on the front waist band and metal clips for the suspenders. They are both fun to wear and, for the occasion that suits.

I've a selection of bras but have somehow come to the conclusion for me, a full cup large size bra is to my liking not only to produce a larger bust like that of the fuller figured lady, but to also cover up my in-fills as I don't like to see them either sticking out of the side or underneath as this totally spoils the effect when looking / admiring myself in the mirror. I've only two colours, black and white and my really preferred bra is a long, Triumph Doreen 42DD cup in white. It's just so perfect and very comfortable to wear and always looks good regardless what clothes I wear on top. I've some mid bras in both colours and, some normal type bras but again, all full cup.

When looking through the racks in M&S not long back, I was quite taken by a 42DD cup padded bra which looked quite big and I thought I'd give it a try. Well we I really disappointed!, It didn't seem to fit at all well and the shoulder straps were uncomfortable in spite of looking OK, then the pads that for the front of the cups constantly stuck up making their own shape and I couldn't get my in-fills to stay put for long. It was nice to try, however not for me and I changed it for a nice regular full cup in white with a lacy trim. Fastening a bra is a sensation I like, it somehow gives me the feeling of being supported and looking good to. All my bras are back fastening and this is fine as I've perfected the art of fastening them behind my back may years past. As I keep saying, this all adds to the fun of dressing in ladies clothes, in particular, under clothes.

If I feel the need to fully dress, the usual type of clothes I like are again the ones that you'd see a mature, full figured lady wear. Some men like to dress in young ladies clothes, even to take on the tarty look and uniform dressing; this is an individual choice but not something that I've ever chosen to do. Real life normal every day clothes are my preference as they were worn by ladies who taught me in school right through to today, and they look great! I've seen the French Maid dressing outfits from time to time in the shops that sell joke clothes and party outfits, however a close look reveals they are sort of a 'one time only outfit' and are not really designed for anything other than a few hours for the occasion. I like reality and relating what I do in everyday life to real time situations. If I chose to dress in a full, ladies outfit then I usually chose a nice blouse to start with, something made from satin or other similar material that's nice to the touch and will fit my figure of 42DD size. Sometimes I'll choose a stretchy polar neck jersey as these really do cling to you figure and bring out the full shape of my bust which I find important. I'll also chose a set of beads, something simple and fitting for the occasion as these along with some matching earrings can really set myself off and, the joy of looking in the mirror to see myself, me all dressed in these clothes and accessories is an experience only to be felt when you actually dress. Those little extras all add to the sensation and making me look like the woman I very much like looking like. For a skirt, usually I like floaty type skirts with pleats and something with a bit of a swish. Wearing a woolen kilt is fine, however there is nothing quite like the sensation of having a satin skirt floating about and swishing against stockings, it's just wonderful and again, all part of the fun and sensation of dressing. As for colours, I really don't mind and have a selection from floral bright patterns through to black evening wear. As for dresses, again I like the same type of materials and, they have to fit my body with a good degree of comfort and, good looks.

Once dressed in a skirt and blouse, or a dress I always like to finish off with a pair of heels. Over the years I've learnt some of the art of wearing and more so walking in heels which is not easy if you don't know how. I've a few pairs of court shoes with 3. ½" heels and these are easy to walk around in and, bring the 'high heel effect' to my look which again brings a sensational and pleasing feeling and appearance. As for colours, I've two black and one red pair and they look stunning with the right outfit. Indeed, I'll sometimes just chose to dress in a full set of my underwear and a pair of heels, the effect really finishes me off looking and feeling good. I've one pair of 4" sling back heels which are sort of very open toed and strappy, however to walk in them is something I've yet to master and, I don't want to end up with a broken ankle! As I talked about dressing the other evening, sometimes I'll wear a pair of heels with my underwear and dressing gown as they add to the effect and, I very much enjoy the short walks from the front room to the kitchen to make a drink as our floors are tiled and the sound of heels clicking, well that's another sensation to behold especially when your dressed and making the noise!

I've no other clothes in my small underwear selection really other that a nice selection of knickers. These I find a lovely thing to buy when out shopping and the mood strikes. I've many pairs from the ones I described from my choice the other evening through to long legged lacy French Style, ordinary full gusset cotton and even some long bloomers in a varied choice of colours. Some evenings, or when I have the opportunity, I'll take a few pairs of knickers out and place them on our bed and one by one, wear them and admire how they fit my body and how I look in them. It gives me the opportunity to understand how they feel and how they will be best suited to an outfit. Obviously the shape of a lady in comparison with a man's body is different however, there is such a selection of knickers available, the space in the right places on some provide the support and looks you need. Again, satin is my favourite choice of fabric, and close to my skin this brings a wonderful feeling. In my early years when I first tried on a girdle and stockings, I didn't try on any knickers until many years later. It's a sensation not to be missed as anyone who wears them will tell you! They are not too expensive to buy and if you get fed up of them and want a change or, to add to your collection they're available in many shops and a good small thing to pick up when shopping and the mood suits.

Now, that's my explanation of how I like to dress in ladies clothes and, I'll share more evenings, afternoons I've spent dressing and changing in order that perhaps you can understand the enjoyment I get from it all. I've yet to talk about hair and makeup as I preferred to keep them separate, however every facet of the subject has varying degrees of interest for me and, I'm sure some men who dress may even find my account of the whole subject and experience, somewhat boring, but this is me. I'm more than happy with my life and all of the years of private pleasure it's brought for me. Indeed I do feel a certain privilege for having this wonderful desire and like so many things in this wonderful world, they are all open to abuse and result is less acceptable practices as I've pointed out in previous chapters.

Do you think I'm weird or strange? Or even a dirty old man? The choice is yours and I'm not writing this to try and convenience anyone it's 'OK and the right thing to do', far from it! I live a perfectly normal average life with perhaps more privileges than many people having the ability to travel and see the world, children and grandchildren, friend and family and all of those material things that aren't that important, but do add to a simpler and more comfortable life style.

Do I connect dressing with a desire for sex? No! You may find that difficult to believe but it's true. I've a wonderful sex life, probably an envy of many and that's my personal business between my wife and me and I've no wish to share any of that with anyone. It's totally a private thing and that's the way it should be in our opinion.

Do I like to look at other men dressed in ladies clothes? Yes from time to time I do, however I must add here that it's for the same reason as I look at myself in the mirror when I'm dressing or fully dressed. It's the fun of seeing how I look in ladies clothes and the wonderful feelings that the whole scenario brings from shopping and deciding which clothes to buy, through to putting them on and feeling the effects of the materials against my flesh. There is a whole host of photos available on Flicker and other web pages, many are of men exposing themselves when dressing in ladies clothes and entering into sex acts. If at any point I find the web pages I've been looking at start down this road, it just turns me off and I've no interest to look any further. Some men look better than others and as a mark out of ten, ten being the highest and one being the lowest, I would rate my looks and appearance as a seven or even eight sometimes for looks and style. My facial features are not too prominent and as a result with some makeup and a hair piece, it takes a second glance from a reasonably short distance to recognize the fact that I'm a man.

I enjoy being a man and wouldn't change it for all of the underwear in the world, or tea in China as my father used to say. I'm a man who likes to dress in ladies clothes from time to time and enjoy everything that goes with them, after that, nothing!

These are some of the adverts that I used to admire as a youngster almost fifty plus years ago. If my memory serves me right the Platex bra was just coming out than and was obviously a big hit with the ladies. There was one called the 'cross your heart bra', I wonder if that still exists today?

Chapter 9

Hair & make up

Moving into hair and makeup brings a whole new perspective to dressing as it really starts to transform you from a man wearing ladies clothes to a man who is starting to look more and more, like a woman!

Have I tried makeup? Yes! Did I like it? Yes! Have I tried a hair piece? Yes! Did I like it? Yes! Yes in fact to all four questions. From that early age I'd really only been interested in ladies underwear and the feeling and sensation it brought to me. Those feelings are exactly the same today as that day long ago after the football match when I'd had a bath. Nothing has changed! The excitement and thought of dressing in ladies clothes still brings that feeling of satisfaction and joy, that warm feeling inside.

Before the days of the internet, I used to pick up a copy of the Exchange and Mart magazine as there was always something to look through in there that appealed to my interest in mechanical things, car parts, engine parts and a whole host of other items. I suppose I'd be at the age of twenty three or four when I would sometimes in the evening or when on holiday read it from cover to cover as opposed to just going straight to the pages I was interested in. There were and probably still are adverts from ladies clothes, hair pieces and a whole host of party and fancy dress items and this brought a certain intrigue for me. Indeed, I wanted to learn more and read deeper and found that there was even companies providing dressing services for men who wanted to change into ladies clothes in privacy. Given that from an early age I realized that I had this desire, feeling, want and erg to dress, I'd never spoken to anyone about it and, didn't even think anyone would certainly cater for what I had as a personal and deeply private interest. However, there where companies out there and this lead me to believe that I was not the only man with this feeling, there are obviously others and judging by the adverts, many others!

I never made an issue out of these adverts and really they would only attract my interest if I'd buy a copy of the E&M. Then in Sunday newspapers [not that I'm a big newspaper reader!], I'd find the odd advert for hair pieces for ladies and men, yet they only indicated that they were for lady styles and this too intrigued me. Again, I didn't make much of it all but somehow knew I was not alone in my likings for this subject, far from it as it was becoming increasingly obvious that there were many other men out there with varying degrees of interest in the wearing of ladies clothes.

It wasn't until I was in my thirties when I decided to buy and try a hair piece and, some make up. By this time, I'd seem many adverts and understood the increasing awareness of the men who wanted to extend their sexual desires and dress up as a lady to become more attracted to men of a similar interest. This did and still does nothing for me. It's my person individual choice and I've no incline or interest in men other than as friends or working colleagues. The 'sex thing' really turns me off actually, but that's me, I'm attracted to the opposite sex and feel very happy and contented about this, it's just somehow natural and something that I've never questioned.

The thought of wearing a hair piece or wig as they are sometimes called really started to appeal to me and, I would see them from time to time when out shopping and look at the different styles. At this point in time I was terrified to go into a shop and pick up an article of ladies clothing let alone a wig! So, I did the next best thing at the time and wrote off to one of the adverts in the Exchange and Mart and they sent back their leaflet of wigs which they had one offer. There were many styles to choose from all in different colours and the prices varied greatly. Which one would I chose? I was totally lost as really, I just fancied putting one on for a try and had no real style I wanted to follow.

I looked at that brochure for many months and could never make up my mind. Quite by chance, I was shopping and had picked up everything I wanted and was heading back toward the car. As a sort cut, I decided to cut through the market hall and came across a stall with loads of different wigs and they were at prices that even if I tried one and didn't like it, I could through it away or, put it in a charity shop bag. I stopped and was having a look when the lady who ran the stall came from behind her counter and said "hello, can I help you?" I was sort of embarrassed and didn't really know how to answer her and said, "I'm just having a look thank you" She said she'd got every style and colour you could think of as she'd just taken delivery of a large order. Her approach was very relaxed and didn't put me on the spot to make a purchase. Plucking up courage, I said, "that black one with shoulder length hair looks good" She picked it off the model and then gave it a brush and handed it to me to look at. I was really nervous at this point and said it was for a fancy dress and that I'd never worn one before. She said it was really to go for a fancy dress one off, however it was up to me. To my astonishment, she asked if I'd like to try it on! I was both gob smacked and pleased as I was really intrigued to understand what it would feel and look like.

"Come through here" she said and I followed putting my shopping down when she handed me the wig and said, 'let me give you a hand'. She explained that there is knack to putting on a wig, let me show you. She told me to tip my head forward and before I knew what was happening, she said "now tip your head back, and look in the mirror!" I was totally shocked! There was me shopping, and now standing here wearing a wig, a shoulder length black wig with curls on the ends of the hair. "Well, what do you think?" she asked and somehow I answered, "I think I look good" and had meant to say, it looked good! She answered agreeing and said it really suite me and proceeded to brush up the curls. It was an amazing experience and again, something I've never forgotten and needless to say, I bought the wig!

That was my first wig and I had some fun wearing it and, kept if for several years until I ruined it by combing it to hard and actually started to pull the hair out of the skull cap. The sensation of wearing the hair piece or wig which ever you prefer to call them is not something that I crave over. Compared with wearing a bra or suspender belt and stockings are, on a scale of one to ten, about two would describe my liking for them. Yes they are nice to wear and it brings yet another dimension to dressing in ladies clothes by adding another 'something else to wear' however, a wig is only an add-on for me.

Trying on makeup is something that I didn't do until I was in my late thirties and, I think this was only because the opportunity didn't arise. I'd certainly thought about it and looked at lipsticks and eye shadow, false lashes and foundation cream, however somehow one is no good without the other and I just didn't bother buying some and as a result, didn't get to wear any. Then one day, I bought some lipstick and then other makeup bits and bobs with the intention of having a try. I'd no intention to try my new found accessory to dressing when I was dressed, instead I thought I'd give it a go while just dressed in my man clothes. One afternoon with the house empty, I went into the bathroom and had a shower and shave, then all clean and bare skin I proceeded to put on my foundation cream. This I found a messy business, however following the instructions, I worked it into my face and let it dry off. Then I put on some eye blue shadow which was good fun and looked quite realistic. Again I found this to be messy stuff and realized the need to have lots of tissues and, face wipes around just in case. After that, I put on some eye liner and mascara which really is art in itself as you can easily poke yourself in the eye and, if you avoid this then the opportunity to make a mess is easy and when I say a mess, I mean a mess! Eye liner is good for making a distinctive line between your shadow and your eye and if applied properly looks really effective. With the entire make up that I'd put on in place, I decided to apply my lipstick as a last and final touch. I'd chosen a dark red which is a really nice colour.

Holding my lips in a sort of open and firm position, I firstly applied the lipstick to my bottom lip and then to the top lip. In order to try and make an appealing shape I applied more and more until in the end, my lips looked huge and standing back from the mirror then having a good look, I feel I'd of frightened the living daylights of anyone who would have seen me literally plastered in make up! What a mess! I realized there and then there must be an art to put make up on successfully and this is obvious or should I say was at that time obviously something I didn't possess. What a waste, however you live and learn as they say! I washed my face several times to remove the lipstick and the staining it had caused and, made sure every speck was removed and no traces of any make up existed on my face and neck. With my face all clean, I set about cleaning the wash basin as the mess from washing it all off had left a ring of scum around the bowl. Scrubbing it off the basin came up nice and clean and I placed all of the makeup and wipes, tissues in a plastic bag, tied the ends together and disposed of it in the bottom of our dust bin. It was many years later before I had another go, this time with a greater degree of satisfaction.

Similarly to wearing a wig, if you ask me to mark my feelings for wearing make up in comparison to wearing underwear, with ten the greatest and one the least, I would say it ranks about four for me. It's a personal choice and, each to their own. If anyone one had walked in on me during that first try on session, they would have jumped out of their skin with fright! Since that time and the introduction of the computer age, I've studied several U Tube pages about applying makeup and false eye lashes and for certain, it's an art and something you can only practice to become good at. I bought lipsticks from time to time and just experimented with them see how my lips would look. My natural lips shape is such that I don't have a very pronounced type of lip, in fact they are sort of narrow and small in comparison with the models you see in ladies magazines. One of the secrets I discovered is to apply a little at a time, by doing this you can stand back and admire your work and, work you lips in order that the lipstick can settle and spread a little. Gently rubbing your lips together also helps to smudge then a little and smoothen out and imperfections. There are all sorts of new lipsticks available today and for certain, the more you're willing to pay, the better the quality and the better the results. Yes it is an art applying makeup; lipstick in particular, however having good quality lippy makes all of the difference. Similarly, foundation creams have changed immensely and there are so many good quality products available today, you need to do some research to understand what to buy to suit your dressing desires and requirements.

Have I worn make up and looked really good? Yes. Was I dressed in my ladies clothes at the time? Yes. Did I wear my wig at the same time? Yes. All in all I have on a few occasions worn everything at once and, I really enjoyed the experience. It was good fun but one thing I noticed was the fact that I was transforming myself into someone else. This may sound silly, however for the first time I saw myself as someone different. Different to the young boy who's inquisitive mind lead him to try on stockings and girdle, but that was somehow different to dressing in full makeup and all of the trimmings. It made me feel different and, I wasn't really sure that I liked it at the time when I dressed. The excitement was wonderful and the results were really good, in fact I amazed myself at how good and realistic I looked. A fuller figured woman with a large bust and pronounced bottom, earrings dangling and a hair neatly brushed, lips shining and eyes neatly shadowed, standing in a skirt and blouse with beads around my neck and 3.1/2 heels. Under those clothes I had everything on I've described in previous chapters, I was amazed and it was a brilliant experience, but was it right for me?

Chapter 10

How far do I go?

For anyone who has the desire to dress in ladies clothes, there is always the nagging question amongst all of the excitement and feelings associated with dressing, 'how far do I go?' It's a very simple question and something that I have asked myself many times over the years and, I've answered that question. I believe it's important as you can then plan what you wish to achieve out of the whole dressing scenario.

It may sound silly to try and pose such a question, however you have to remember you're actually doing something different, something that not everyone will agree to and, in some cases doing something that many people totally disagree with and, sadly to say this appears to the be the vast majority of the population. Is it right for a man to dress in ladies clothes? Well apparently the law says it's OK provide there are valid reasons, however as I've stated in my first to chapters, if you're the average normal type of guy who were to be caught, seen dressed perhaps on ladies clothes then, there would be a question posed for your motive.

Even the closest of friends and family, your partner of wife would really find this behavior strange and want to know why you're doing this?

Up until today, there is no conclusive answer to the question. It's a mystery that has yet to be solved and hopefully this book will bring another shred of light on the subject for people to read and understand more, for those well qualified to analyses and perhaps pick up on some snippet of information and help them piece the complex jigsaw puzzle together to see the entire picture. I certainly don't have all of the answers, however being involved in the subject for many years and, having the patients to write and go to print about my feelings and experiences may help find those missing pieces.

When I say 'how far do you / I go?', it's with valid reason I say this as there are many paths off this road you can go down, some knowingly, some willingly and, some by mistake which will bring regret and damage to your entire remaining life! Life is to be enjoyed and it's a very precious gift that we need to preserve. Living a happy and normal life can be turned upside down in a few second by something that happens which, is beyond your control. It can be for the better or, for the worst and obviously we all avoid that 'for the worse' scenario as much as possible.

If you go to Google and look for information to help you understand your desire to dress in ladies clothes, you'll find literally thousands and thousands of pages to read thanks to Google's search engine capability. There are articles to read that cover nearly every facet of the subject, however there is one common trend and that's to add a name for the person who is dressing in ladies clothes as though to categorize you, put you in a box and have a large 'tick' alongside. I'm sure by now obviously with your interest in the subject you've looked at these web pages and understand what I'm talking about.

The dressing in ladies clothes in many, perhaps most cases is just a necessity for some men as it's an extension of their other desires and these men are also give names by category. Wearing of ladies clothes to them is a way of life and some have gone to and continue to change their whole life which is a huge commitment and I really applaud their devotion and reasoning behind their plight. Others just wish to extend their sexual experiences and attract others who enjoy those same experiences. At this point you really have to give some thought as to 'what do I really want to achieve out of dressing and, how far do I want to go?'

This may sound as though I'm complicating a simple desire and making a big issue out of it all. Perhaps I am, but with valid reason and for your benefit if you're either already starting to dress or, dressing and wondering 'how far should I go?' There are varying degrees that bring each individual the satisfaction that he wishes to achieve and as with everything in life. Somehow, man's inquisition within himself will make him want is bigger, faster, higher, deeper and to push the envelope out to reach the untouchable. It's a natural 'built in' aspect for many men, men who have explored far flung places both on this earth and up into the atmosphere. However there are some limits to everyone's desire and tolerance for a particular subject and I believe that men 'dressing in ladies clothes' is, one of them.

If I was to put myself in one of the many boxes and place a tick alongside it, the best description of me and my desires would be termed as a cross dresser. It somehow seems to be the mildest of descriptions as all of the others really indicate a connection with sex such as transsexual, transvestite and so on. As I've stated throughout my chapters, not in any way do I connect my dressing habits, desires, experiences, sensations with sex, it just doesn't even enter my head to think about the subjects as for me, they are not connected. For others, there are serious connections and they as I've stated earlier, use the dressing just as a part of their desire.

So, I'm a cross dresser if that's the box I'm to be placed in and that's fine by me. It actually takes a lot of courage to admit to being called such a type of person and, that's something that needs to be recognized as this whole subject does take varying degrees of courage to admit to. Later, I'll take about 'others in my life' and you'll then why I am putting so much emphasis on this simple question, 'how far do I go'. It's important at some stage to really give this some thought as if not, then you can end up strolling down a road of life with no return! Let me explain.

As an average guy, well that's how I would describe myself with all of the usual happenings and things in life, what too they say? "Married with two point four children, a mortgage for twenty five years and holiday abroad at least once a year!" Perhaps this has changed now statistically, however I'm sure you know what I'm implying here. This 'normal and happy, contented' way of life that perhaps you take for granted can change dramatically if someone finds out that you're a cross dresser! That simple desire to perhaps wear a pair of knickers, a bra or whatever if taken for a few minutes and you're seen by some one, your wife, your partner, your friend or close acquaintance can lead them to think the worst. Somehow in this day and age it's an automatic reaction, to think that you're doing this for some weird and perverted reason where really, you were probably just being curious. The results though in those split seconds can have a devastating effect on your future life. Even the most tolerant of people see a man dressing in ladies clothes as 'really out of the box actions' and regardless of how you explain you're reasoning, they somehow have this nagging question in the back of their mind, 'why did he want to do that?'

You can brush it off and say it was only for fun, it was only something I wanted to do to see what you'd say, it was only because I didn't have any other clean clothes to I thought I'd borrow some of yours, the excuses are endless! Fact is that you have been seen in ladies clothes and, that some one knows about it and, they might even tell someone else about if they're of that type of person and then it opens Pandora's Box! You're suddenly branded in one form or another as a guy who dresses in ladies clothes. It's strange but true, people immediately brand you as a pervert, and think the worst for your actions and even to the extent people may see you as a threat to society. Yes it's as simple or serious as that and is this something you're willing to go through? Remember at this point I'm only talking about being seen by someone wearing only a pair of knickers! Can you imagine if you're seen fully dressed what those same people will and do think?

At this point again I must stress that I'm not here to advise what is wrong or right on this subject, what you should or shouldn't do as these are actions for which you have your own thoughts and responsibilities. If you're interests are in having sexual experiences and people already know of your likings, tendencies and desire and that's fine by you then, it's your life and do with it as you will. For those who are just simply curious and want to further their curiosity and desire to try on some clothes, think about it, is it really worth it? Is it worth you risking of being found out if no one knows of your interest and desire?

For certain, and I would think that most men regardless of if they are single or married at some point in their lives have picked up a pair of knickers and thought, "I wonder what those feel like to wear?" I know I did, and that was at an early age! But somehow even then I felt that it was something I had to be careful about who I would share my feelings and thoughts with, something I enjoyed but realized that there really was no one at that point in my life I could share such intimate thoughts with. This lead me to the conclusion I should keep it to myself and feel happy knowing I have this tendency, desire and urge to dress in ladies clothes.

In knowing this, understanding the 'perhaps' consequences it's always made me think before acting as to understand that 'what if's' about my action should they be found out. If at that early age I'd of chosen not to open that laundry basket lid to see what that dangling strap was attached to hanging over the side, would it have made any difference to my life as it is? I probably think not. Would it have made me a better or bad person? Would it have made me to have no interest at all in ladies clothes? I very much doubt this. Perhaps if it wasn't at that time when the garment in question, a girdle and some stockings really took my fancy, it would have happened again later on. What's done is done and you can't turn back those pages, more over would I want to turn them back and have my life done differently? No, not for one minute and I have no regrets at all, in fact I believe my life to be the envy of many!

That being said, remembering I'm just an average man, in size, weight, colour and thoughts, I do very much value my life and under no circumstances would I risk changing this for anything. My life is not only about me, me is part of my life and my life is my wife, a lady who I love dearly and wouldn't do anything knowingly in the world to either hurt her or, break of love and trust. When we got married some thirty six years ago, we both said some words in front or witnesses and come hell or high water we both uphold those words, of love and trust. They are important, in fact very important and something we don't knowingly or willing abuse and if in some way we do, then we rectify the wrong in whatever form that takes to uphold our wonderful marriage. Everyone who's married or in a relationship knows only too well that you share each other's most intimate thoughts and desires knowing full well they will go no further. Whether you both agree with them is another subject, however having this wonderful privilege is something that should be honored and preserved.

If you're single, then you've probably got some friends, family or relatives who you're close to and by the same token, there's usually a mutual respect for those people in your life. You respect their thoughts and opinions and perhaps you have one who you're closer to that anyone else, someone you can confide in, someone who you trust and they trust and respect you. Would you like to have this trust broken? Would it hurt you to know your 'trusted friend or partner' was doing something that you didn't know about and or agree with, I think that answer is yes, it would!

I have always had this desire to dress, and I believe somehow that it will remain with me for the rest of my life and, that's fine. What I've been able to do, is to come to terms with it and enjoy it in a controlled fashion. Yes, sometimes I feel that I'd perhaps like to go out for a walk dressed in my entire splendor, however would it be worth the risk of being spotted by someone who knows me? Would it be worth risking some fifty years of life, a good life and good reputation for being the person I am? Or at least, the person I am without my desires to dress in ladies clothes, the answer is no! Definitely not!

So, it's up to the individual how far you actually want to go, not perhaps an easy question to answer but for certain, one that needs some consideration. Consideration not only for you, but for the people around you who think a lot of you and, hold you in there dearest thoughts.

If you're somehow looking to extend your fantasies for some sexual full filment then again, whatever lights you candle as they say and not for me to comment on. Coming back to my thoughts and explanations toward how far do you want to go, if I can offer advice its simple. Don't do anything which you're really unsure about and certainly don't set out to deceive or offend anyone, it wouldn't be worth it. If you can be certain that you really need to try on some clothes then do so, but make sure you're not going to be discovered or found out and then see how you feel. If you're married or living with your partner and are unsure as to what to do, then think about sharing your desires with them and see if they will support you. Don't expect an immediate supportive 'oh yes go ahead' as I don't think even for the most understanding person this will be their reaction.

Just because you're full of the feelings and desire doesn't mean others are, in fact it's going to come as a shock and surprise to them so be aware that you're going to most lightly receive some resistance to even have a conversation about the subject let alone, to have someone's approval. I've been through this and will explain my experience with the whole thing of sharing for the first time in my life, my desire and feelings to want to dress in ladies clothes. It's not been an easy road for me to travel, that being said being married to the most wonderful lady in the whole world has certainly made me realize how fortunate I am. Not all people are the same and I can after being through this, see and understand exactly the reaction of a loving wife when she is broached with the subject from her husband, "I want to dress up in knickers, bra and stocking dear!" It must hit her like a brick wall!

To have been married to the guy you rely on as man, a man who sorts out problems, be it a blocked drain, money, work, the washing machine that doesn't work, children when they become a handful, the death of a family member or friend and to be that man in her life to suddenly realize that this man is now perhaps a sissy, well it doesn't take a brain surgeon to realize this news is devastating and, stops the person in her tracks dead!

The fact that you're telling her will immediately bring doubts of your mutual trust and love, it opens up so many things to think about including for her, "what did or didn't I do for you?" It brings questions toward sex and your relationship as for certain and as I've mentioned before, somehow dressing in ladies clothes isalways associated with wanting to gain more out of a sexual fantasy or, to achieve something that you're not already getting out of your relationship with your partner or wife. Can you imagine how that must feel? It must bring the feeling of, "I'm not good enough, I've not done something, and I thought everything was perfect and now????" Do you really want to put your loved one or partner though all this? No, it's not fair and you need to provide some consideration and decide if you are to share your desire, how you're going to broach the subject and why.

If you do and there's any incline of an understanding for your thoughts and desires, then the next immediate logical question will be, "how far do you want to go?" The knowing of something even if it's not good news is much better to cope with than the not knowing. We all like to know and it needs careful consideration before making any commitments or promises.

So, have a think about the whole subject. I've thought about it hundreds of times and even pushed it back to the furthest part of mind and shut it out for months, even years and tried desperately to ignore it when the feeling came back, however one thing is for certain, it never goes way and perhaps you could / would say that's the sign of a weak character. Men are not as strong character wise and women, that's a fact and surrendering to my desire, having been through the "should I", "shouldn't I" situation time and time again more so in recent years [the past twenty], I came to realize that this desire is both a blessing and sometimes a curse! A blessing for all of the sensations and pleasures it brings, a curse for all the turmoil it creates in your mind when you've many other things to get on with and think about in life.

It's really only something simple, however the consequences of your actions can bring pleasure, it can also bring devastation and pain! Again, I stress to anyone thing about 'having a go' to give consideration to what you're really wanting to achieve and, how far you want to go. If you can't answer these questions all be them not perhaps fully, then don't go any further. Leave it and give it some more thought and force yourself to provide an honest answer. I say this as some time back, when you could openly chat on MSN, I was talking with a guy of similar age and what I thought were similar desires and we would chat from time to time on the subject for which we both had the same desires. It was interesting to hear his feelings and thoughts and while I was totally discrete and from our first conversation, made it plain that I had no sexual interest or desire toward the subject. He, some month later in what I presumed was mutual understanding and respect for one and other for which I'd made it clear, he asked if we could meet up and 'spend the night together?' I was totally shocked and replied back that I was really surprised by his request and that I'd made it plain I'd no interest in this type of subject. He apologized and said that he's always had hidden feelings toward wanting a relationship with another man, even though he said he was happily married. Confusing or what?

Being prepared to deal with such requests needs to be clear in your mind as supposing that same request came to you and quite innocently you agreed to meet that man and, it turned out he was different to what you expected and had different expectations of the outcome. You in all innocents would feel totally embarrassed and disappointed that someone had abused you confidence in them. On the other had if you've had this desire for some time and wish to meet other men, and that's entirely up to you. It's your choice and only you can make that choice.

If you have no interest in this facet of life similar to me, then I would add that even though perhaps your desire to dress is only that, to put on some garments of ladies clothes and experience the wonderful feeling that it brings, keep it to yourself or, share it with your loved one or partner before doing so. I've dressed on my own without my wife's knowledge in the past and, even on one occasion she came home and found me, fully dressed in everything including a wig and make up! I'll explain about this in the coming chapters.

In summary, there is no definitive answer as to 'how far should I go', but something that needs some thought and, keep in mind what you want to achieve and why. If you're up front and honest with yourself, then you'll find the answer you're looking for and, hopefully this will lead to the satisfaction you desire. I'm a fortunate man as; I have found my answer and have realized how contented I am with the outcome.

Chapter 11

Shopping

*N*ow here is a part of dressing in ladies clothes that I find very interesting and, very satisfying. Over the years, I've probably done and experienced every type of shopping for clothes that's been available and I'll share these with you. For those of you who already dress, then I'm sure you'll have a chuckle and remember similar circumstances! It's all part of the learning curve as they say and after you've learnt a thing or two, then such experiences are actually laughable and you then wonder 'what was all the fuss about?'

Before the wonderful days of the internet and internet shopping, you had not much choice other than to front up at a shop and select what you wanted to purchase and take it to the shop assistant who would place it in a bag and you could then make payment. The first few times I went to do this, I actually failed! Yes I went with the objective of making a purchase of some stockings and was to say the least, 'trembling like a leaf' in case anybody saw me or even worse, asked me 'who those were for? Silly isn't it, but true! I gave up and walked out of the shop both disappointed and feeling really silly as what was there to be nervous about? Everything, at the time!

I've always been the type of person who is confident in most situations and sometimes even amaze myself how I can take control and the lead role if the circumstances demand, particularly at work. I was still a single guy at the time and just felt the need to wear some stockings. I'd of liked a suspender belt to hold them up, but one step at a time I thought, let's make a purchase of the simple thing first, stockings!

The only place I could think of that immediately came to mind to buy some stockings was M&S. We don't live to far away from our local store, it's about ten miles and, one Saturday afternoon I set off to make my purchase. All went well and I was brimming with confidence and walked through the store and came across the ladies under wear or 'lingerie' section as it's referred to, today. Sure enough there were many flat packs of stockings to choose from and I was intrigued by the colours and wondering about sizes. It actually came to mind then, how or what did the sizes of stockings look like? Did they go by length? If so I had not got a clue and had no idea as to what size I would need!

So as not to draw to much attention to myself, [me being the only man looking through the ladies underwear section] I moved away from the stockings or hosiery as it's referred to and found some girdles which looked very interesting and at this point, I thought how very much I'd like to buy one of these as it would serve to hold up my stockings. I started to feel quite confident and relaxed and picked up a white girdle and began looking at the fastening and, the suspenders. It only had four but at that time I'd no idea whether four, six or eight were the better option, I just wanted to try on some stockings.

Looking at the label, I was just about to start studying the size when a shop assistant who I'd not noticed had obviously been watching me and came over to see if she could help. "Is everything all right?" she asked and I froze! Yes froze! Holding a girdle I didn't know how to answer her and came out with a stuttering "I was just looking for the size". She took the garment off me and said it was a large and then asked what size I was looking for. I said I didn't really know as it was for someone else and she asked me who? At this point I didn't know what to say and said "it doesn't matter right now as I'll have to ask the person her size" She smiled and put the garment back on rack and asked if there was anything else she could help with? At this point with a bright red face, I said "no thanks" and walked out of the shop. What a fool I felt and how stupid I felt at the same time. My heart was racing and I wondered if she was thinking it was for me? Perish the thought, may be she'd of told her manager that a young man was wanting to buy some ladies underwear, would I ever be able to go back and shop there again? Stupid, but true!

I had a walk around just browsing other similar shops to see if they sold stockings and found a 'ladies underwear' shop that specialized in exactly what I was looking for. Looking through the window, the display of underwear was very interesting and I'd of liked very much to have gone and looked through the items for sale which included lots of girdles, corsets, bras and all of the interesting things I'd seen many years before when looking through the catalogues, I mentioned earlier. There on display where some flat pack stockings, 'Pretty Polly' I seem to remember was the make / brand and it said tan colour in denier number … whatever that was. Again I had no idea what denier meant and wondered about the sizing. May be if I said they were for my mother as a present, I could describe her size and an assistant would offer help. I plucked up the courage and went into the shop to find the assistants all busy with ladies making their purchases. If I think back, to have had a few hours to look through all of the underwear in the shop, it would have been a wonderful experience as there seemed to be every single type of ladies underwear you could think of on display and, I would only imagine what would have been in those draws under the counter and in the stock room. It would have been pure delight just to look.

I was nervous from my last experience only some thirty minute previous but somehow, I seemed to regain my composure so to speak when a lady assistant in a very stern voice said "and what does Sir want?" Again, I froze and this lady was of the type that I remember is school who would issue a hundred lines if you dared make the wrong reply! I said that I wanted to buy my mother a present, some stockings and wanted them in a tan colour. She looked at me then turned away and walked toward the counter and I thought she was going to pick some out for me to look at. Wrong! She stood behind the counter and suggested that my mother come to the shop and, 'purchase her own stockings', *then she could choose the ones she wanted and I could pay for them! Talk about having the wind knocked out of your sails, by this time my interest in ladies underwear had really diminished! Needless to say I looked no further and gave the whole idea up at that point just too hard to do. The lady somehow didn't believe my motive for shopping and perhaps my nervous approach gave her some sort of suspicion, that the stockings where perhaps not for my mother.*

Those days of shopping like that are thankfully gone as for certain, if a shop assistant had treated me in such an abrupt manner as the one in the ladies underwear shop, I am sure if I'd have requested to see the person in charge, she would have been asked to apologize and be a little more helpful.

Quite conversely, only this last December I was shopping in M&S as they have opened a new store not too far from where we live and I believe it's one of the most modern and 'ecofriendly' stores in the country and, the selection of ladies clothes including underwear is just huge to say the least. Both my wife and I were doing some shopping and generally out for a wander and thought M&S would be a great place to start. We had a look around and truthfully you spend the full day looking at of what they have on display. We agreed to split up and meet later for a coffee and some lunch, so off I wandered into the underwear section. The range is just huge, however not everything on display is to everyone's liking and was looking for a full cup bra and some nice knickers.

Looking through the full cup bra section, I found the ones I was looking for and they really looked the part that is a nice wide back straps, good shoulder straps, full cups with nice lacy material and four hook and eye back fasteners. I looked through the sizes and was looking for a 42 DD, however I could only find D or G sizing in the 42. An assistant was tidying the racks and asked if she could help and I said I was looking for a 42DD in this particular style. She took the number of the tag and said she'd go and check and sure enough after a few minutes she returned with the exact one I was looking for. "Brilliant" I said, 'that's pleasing as its perfect". She said that was good and was there anything else she could help me with. My reply was that I was going to have a look for some matching knickers in the same sort of style. She said there are some on the rack over there pointing me in the right direction. I thanked her and she said a pleasant "my pleasure, let me know if there's anything else I can help you with". The store wasn't too busy and I had a good look through the knickers section and found a pair which were perhaps not the most exciting but felt lovely and soft and, had the right sort of elastic I like on the legs in order to keep my manly parts in place! Looking through the sizes, I found the one I wanted and was really pleased. By this time the same lady assistant had worked her way over tidying the racks where the knickers were and asked "did you find what you're looking for?" I said "yes thanks, perfect". She said "that's good, as whoever you're buying them for will be pleased however, if they're not right you can bring them back". I told her that they were exactly what I was hoping to buy and that it's nice to pick up everything that you want. Somehow perhaps a little inquisitive, she asked if there was anything else I wanted as there was a rack of sale items to browse through. I walked over to the sale rack and she followed me then picked out a padded bra in the same size and held it up. I looked at it and then took it in my hands for a closer look. It did look interesting and I was tempted to buy it, and somehow I felt that she had already suspected that I was buying the clothes for me. Quite openly I said, "I've never tried a padded bra before, somehow it looks quite large". Without even glancing she said why not try it and if it's not right you can bring it back. Her approach was totally open and helpful. Did she somehow know the items where for me to wear? Who knows, the main thing was her kind and courteous approach. Obviously many years on, my confidence has grown and buying my underwear is a joy and something I like doing very much when I'm in the mood that is. If not, I've no interest what so ever!

The bra was not for me and that's exactly what I did, bought it and brought it back as while it did look interesting, it was far from comfortable and, the padding always seemed to stick up and is obviously made for a lady with a natural large bust which needs support.

The difference in shopping for over the counter underwear is really amazing and is now a pleasurable experience. I suppose as well, over the year, buying presents for my wife from similar department stores has added to my confidence and, it's a real pleasure. Yes I like shopping while I know most men really despise the thought of it. If my wife ever says she wants to go shopping and asks if I'd be interested to come, unless there is something pressing I never miss the opportunity and that doesn't mean I use every occasion to look for underwear and clothes. Sometimes as I say, I've no interest but really like accompanying g her and helping with the shopping trolley or bags. Am I strange for liking this? Well perhaps some would say so, however we like doing things together and rarely tire of each other company and, there's always time to stop and have a drink of tea or coffee on a shopping trip!

I've bought quite a few items of underwear from charity shops in years gone by, however in recent times the racks of secondhand underwear seem to have disappeared, may be due to health and hygiene regulations? Or have the charity shops stopped selling underwear because more men were buying the items than ladies! Obviously some of the items for sale looked used and I'd never contemplate buying such items, however you could often find some garments which had obviously never come out of the draw and never been worn. Old fashioned girdles and corsets have a great fascination for me and I've see some really nice ones from time to time, trouble is that I've not been in the right company or by myself which would have permitted me to make a purchase and going back the following day, sods law, they were always gone! Sometimes quite by chance I've seem items such as girdles for sale in 'ex-catalogue shops' and these are all brand new. Looking through the baskets of goods, usually they are all too often the sizes that don't sell S or XXXL! But not very often sizes that would fit me!

My man sizing is:-

> 16 ½ collar, 42 chest, 38 waist, 8 ½ shoe and 31 leg.

My lady clothes are:-

> *42DD, 38 waist, 40 hips, size 18, size 8 shoe.*

Buying clothes on the internet has made life so easy and there's a much larger range for any type or style you're looking for. Take for instance a suspender belt. As I've stated in previous chapters, the ones offered in the high street shops and department stores are really a joke. They are not meant to be worn for the purpose they are originally designs, but for a lady to have the off flurry in stockings perhaps to please a partner and why not! However if you wear them to hold stockings up on a regular bases you need them to be both comfortable and functional. Deep waist, number of straps, metal clips and adjusters, preferred fastenings and appearance are all important. When I was on that shopping trip in M&S, they had only two on sale, both looked very thin and uncomfortable and, the clips and adjusters were plastic, they would have failed with a quick snatch! You can search as you like and there are countless companies who provide exactly what you're looking for and in any colour you can think of. Type 'eight strap suspender belt' into Ebay, the pages that come up are just endless. You don't have to worry about those fears I used to have of dealing with 'less than helpful' shop assistants and for that matter, you can shop from the comfort of your own home and they deliver to your door. What better way of shopping for ladies clothes is there than that, particularly if you're nervous or perhaps apprehensive of approaching a shop assistant for help.

Most internet shops are really good with returns too! Last December I ordered a suspender belt – eight straps in a size XL as the chart stated XL covers from a 36 to 40 waist. Well, being a 38 waist, I didn't think anymore and placed the order and the garment arrived in the post two days later. It was exactly what I thought it would be and I was pleased until I tried it on. The material was really nice and stretchy, however this was a problem as truly, it would have fitted a 44 waist due to the stretch and as I like my stockings held up quite tightly, the belt would have wandered down my waist while I was wearing it. So with no further ado, I quickly contacted the supplier and asked if they could change it for an M size. They checked stock and said 'no problem'; just return it as quickly as possible in order that they could dispatch the replacement. With Christmas only a few days away, the cut off for posting was actually tomorrow and I somehow doubted even with the best endeavors if would actually arrive before the shutdown. To my surprise, the next day post arrived with the replacement and a wonderful note to say they had posted it, First Class in order to try and ensure it arrived on time. Service or what? They didn't even make any charges for that extra service!

Buying over the internet couldn't be easier. I'd been fancying a lace up corset for quite some time, however they are not available in most high street shops and those that are advertised, are to say the least quite a lot of money and if you're only buying to try, then it can be a waste of money. Yes you can send it back, however it could take you several weeks to decide if you like it or not. The one I was interested in, was an under bust medium to long body with bones and steel fastenings and laces in plain black, no pattern and, the average price was seventy to eighty pounds. Whichever way you look at it, that's a lot of money just for a 'try on session'!

I continued looking and found the exact same item for twenty four pounds on Ebay! Could it be too good to be true, may be! Anyway I made a purchase and the item duly arrived as few days later and, it's perfect! It's exactly what the advert said it was and, the sizing was also correct as many companies vary their size from each other, that's a point to bear in mind, not all XL's are the same size. It fits perfectly and is a joy to wear providing both the shape and excitement and sensation of being wasted in so to speak!

The range of clothes and accessories available today for a man who wishes to dress in ladies clothes or perhaps as ho's referred to as the 'cross dresser' leaves nothing to the imagination. As with everything, someone always seems to go that little bit further and to the next step. Be it in detail or to being something as close to reality as possible. You've listened to me talk about wearing my bras and referring to 'in-fills'. There is literally every type of 'infill' you can imagine available today to satisfy you needs ranging from, simple form triangles to breast forms of ever size and shape resembling a ladies breast. Just type breast form into Ebay for instance and the pages that come up are mind blowing, as the offerings are in the thousands

Over the years I've experiemented with all types of simple items to fill my bra and make the shape I look for. Obviously liking the fuller figured lady with a larger bust, then using a filling that provides the necessary shape is important and, it has to feel right. I've used balloons filled with water and making sure the knot is tied tightly as, a leak causes all sorts of embarrassing discomfort! Experimenting with balloons is fun and advice for anyone starting out and thinking of using them, always chose the largest 'party type balloon as they are large and tougher than the normal size and have less chance of bursting. They are incredibly tough and will only fail if punctured. Filling a balloon should be done with luke warm water, as cold water against your chest really dampens any further desire to have water filled in-fills! Filling to the correct size is just a trial and error process until you reach the desired size. Once both are filled and dried off on a clean towel and, checked for leaks, placing them in your bra cups is good fun as they just mould to the shape of your bra cup. With both in place, you can feel the stain of the weight on your shoulder straps and, it feels somehow realistic although, I'd never try and explain how a lady feels with respect to her bust as only she would be able to provide that explanation.

My liking for balloons changed over the years and I preferred just foam in-fills cut to shape and these can be used time and time again as opposed to balloons why are a 'one time only' use, then they are thrown away. You can again buy foam in fills of any shape and size and they are relatively in expensive and are advertised as breast forms for sleeping in.

Reading about the subject in more recent times, men who like to dress as ladies and have a bust are really attracted to using breast forms which can be, glued to your chest using special tape or adhesives. They come in all shapes and sizes, some with nipples and others with just the shape of a breast. Many feel the weight of the breast is important as it adds to the effect when wearing a bra with weight causing a sort of bounce as you walk, just like the 'real thing!' For me, I've thought about the idea and have to admit they do have a certain appeal, however I came to the conclusion that the underwear and clothes are my interest and using breast forms was going too far. Many men who do chose to use them, like to go braless and show off their breasts, which is their choice, however for me that has no appeal and again, it's just my personal choice.

The other aspect of using breast forms to consider, if you have an understanding partner or wife, who's consented to you wearing some underwear and clothes and, now finds you're wanting false breasts, then for certain she will wonder what your motive will be as they somehow are sex related. Is it the look, the feel you'd be liking, or just to fill your bra shape?

Similarly to breast forms, you can purchase bottom enhancers which you place in your knickers or, you can buy these already sown in and need only to wear them.

Again so many items to choose from and these really are a personal choice and, it all depends on how far you wish to go. Shopping is great fun and the confidence it brings as well really is a good feeling. Somehow today even in the high street stops, assistants seem to be more helpful than in past times and I would say to any man who's wanting to buy some items of clothing, if you're sure this is what you want to do then don't be frightened, it's easy and, it's fun!

My lace up under bust corset, a pure delight to wear and the shapes it creates, well I can't begin to describe it, you'll have to experience it yourself!

Chapter 12

Out and about

In understanding how far you want to go in your dressing desires is important as it will help you to think through and determine the many facets of the subject. Becoming interested is perhaps a natural curiosity for many men, myself included! However, determining how far you want to go will enable you to become realistic with your feelings and desires and understand if there are going to be any limitations.

Speaking from my experiences and going back those early days when my curiosity got the better of me, I tried on a girdle and some stocking and enjoyed every minute of it. As I've explained, those feelings have never left me in spite of the fact that wax & wane from time to time however one thing is for sure, they always return. Walking from the bathroom to the bedroom to admire myself in these new found garments was something I very much enjoyed and, even during those early years I tried to imagine what it would be like to go out and about fully dressed. It was a dream back then as certain from my limited knowledge of the subject and, definitely not wanting to be found out, I had no idea how I could achieve this.

Looking through those catalogues at all of the different underwear and ladies clothes, shoes also took my fancy and during my years growing up in senior school, I very much admired the sound of our lady teachers who used to click clack up and down the tiled corridors of the school. The noise somehow had a fascination and, the shape looked very pleasing, attractive and very feminine. As I've said before, if I was to have shared my thoughts with anyone, who would have this of bean and, would they have told anyone? While underwear was and still is my favourite of all of my dressing desires, wearing a complete outfit also fascinated me then, as it does now. I asked myself the question, 'when I am dressed, what will I do then?' It sort of lead me to the conclusion that if I was to dress in a complete outfit, with all of the trimmings, then maybe I'd desperately want to go out and about dressed in my entire splendor! This concerned me as for a variety of reasons I felt that perhaps, I'd be getting into something which I'd lose control and, I'm not the sort of person who likes that idea. Please understand, in no way am I a control freak! Far from it!

Going our dressed up in a nice skirt swishing against my stockings, feeling all held up and well supported in a girdle or corset, wearing a nice wig and makeup, ensuring my blouse matched my skirt and having matching shoes and a hand bag really had its appeal and, still does. One thing though, once I'd walked out fully dressed, would it be a one off or would it be the first of two, or three, or more? Somehow I could never find the answer to this question.

Looking on U Tube, if you type in 'cross dresser out and about' there are many videos you can look through at men who decided to take the plunge and enter outside of their private world into the open and, make movies of themselves or, have friend or relatives to film them. It's obviously a desire they have feel the need to full fill those feelings. For certain, it may sound silly but there is always a sense of pride from making a movie and or taking some photos and displaying them for others to see. It always comes back to the question, how far do you want to go?

Perhaps many men crave to be dressed in ladies clothes and regardless of their appearance and what others who see them might think, feel so strongly to the point where looks come a second, it's the need to be 'out and about' dressed in ladies clothes to perhaps enjoy the feeling or, to attract other men in order to full fill their sexual desires. It's an individual's choice and not something I'm going to say is wrong or right. It's something only you can make your mind up with.

Yes, I've looked at many of those videos and somehow wonder what the individual concerned is trying to demonstrate or look for. There are ones of men who are dressed and drive out in a car to a discrete lay-by and then set up their camera in order to capture themselves walking up and down on film. Quite often, you'll see a car passing and can tell by their movements that they are not really comfortable and this may be their first time of doing it. There are others who again chose a discrete place in some quiet wood or waste land and set up their camera and stroll up and down then decide to lift their skirt and bare all! Perhaps this is to gain attention to others who 'may come along' and have the same desires? Who knows, however one thing is for certain, they have chosen to come out of their private world and start to venture into our everyday surroundings.

There are others who dress immaculately and either drive themselves out to a park or country side and go for a walk enjoying the quiet and freedom or, amongst other people in order to gain confidence and become more relaxed learning the art of walking and sitting, picking up things you drop by accident and doing all in a discrete and lady like manner. Some look really convincing and, for all intents even look a lot smarter and more attractive than many women in this day and age sad as it is to say.

I've again, after looking at these videos asked me, "I wonder how far this person wants to go?" For the ones who I feel just from my observations, are perhaps wanting to experience the freedom to walk anywhere dressed in ladies clothes, there is a certain attraction that I can relate to. However the implications of being seen by a family member or friend, working colleague or someone who knows you has to be considered as the implications could affect the rest of your life. And at this point, should you have chosen to venture out and enjoyed all of the experience and feeling smug in knowing "you've done it!" then on the way back to the car or even walking to your house, some calls to you and you turn and reply then, they see you dressed in all of your splendor, what then? I'm sure in such an embarrassing situation, you'd perhaps make an excuse and hope it was told well enough for the person to believe, however there would be that nagging doubt always hanging over you and, you'd start with the regrets, "was it really worth it?'

While on holiday many some years back in the Lake District, we'd have a lovely afternoon walking through the forests and woodland by the lake with some very special friend and, decided we'd got out to a local pub for an evening meal and few glasses of something. It was a good idea and on our way back to the car, I spotted some public loos and said I needed to pay a visit before driving off. The ladies agreed and we proceeded in the direction of the loo's splitting to go in the ladies and gents side. The relief of releasing what seemed like pints of water was well needed! While stood there I picked up on some sounds coming from one of the locked cubicles, it was the sound of a man who by all accounts was having some sort of sexual sensation or, that's what it sounded like anyway! I finished by business and was washing my hands when the door opened and a man walked out and then followed by what at a glance looked like a lady. That split second fooled me as even though he didn't turn his head, he was a man in ladies clothes.

He didn't look very convincing even though I only caught a rear glance as he turned hurriedly and disappeared amongst the vehicles in the car park. To say the least, I was shocked and stunned then, when the cold truth appeared in my mind. These guys had obviously been having some sort of sexual 'pleasure' in the toilet of all places. It made my stomach turn over and I really felt sick. My initial thought where 'what if a young boy had wanted the loo and gone in and been confronted by those two?' The effects on a youngster's mind to see that could have had devastating effects, it did with me, a fully gown man!

You're probably thinking, what I am making all this fuss over as they actually never bothered me. True, however that sort of activity I find deplorable and can't tolerate. Men having affairs and even sex in public toilets, it doesn't bare thinking about and again as I type this sentence, it makes my stomach turn. Somehow I just can't come to terms with this and never will. I'm not here to judge, but certain things in life I will not keep silent about and this sort of 'sleazy doings' are one of them.

This brings me to the point that, as I'm a man who dresses in ladies clothes, 'am I' to be put into the same category as that man in the toilets? I certainly hope not! I'm a clean living, respecting married man with all of the natural desires toward the opposite sex and uphold common decency and, respect for others. The fact that if I was to go out and someone did recognize me, it comes to mind that even with the most understanding person, be it a loved one, relative, friend or colleague, they would somehow connect my dressing to the sleazy people who I've described just. Could I live with that? No!!!!!!!

It would be a wonderful situation if by some magic happening, it would be accepted by everyone that a man dresses from time to time in ladies clothes and can be seen out and about without fear of being 'found out'. However, you know as well as I do, that this sort of fantasy is just a fantasy and will remain like that. It's just something that logically can't happen. Yes there are events if so wish to join in with them that accept you being dressed, in fact unless you are you can't attend, however if you've made the decision to be part of this type of group or following then you're already 'out and about'. How you deal with this at home or, amongst friends is for you to decide and I'm sure you'll be happy with your decision.

There are clubs and meeting venues you can visit and join if you so wish and spend time with likeminded people. This may suit you're needs and full fill you're desires and bring you to a conclusion of how far you're willing to go and accept the fun, joy, experience and possible consequences for your actions. Indeed, there are web pages for such clubs and for all intents and purposes, the men and women seem to be enjoying themselves and for that, I really feel pleased and wish them all of the best. There's a part of me that wonders what it would be like, for certain sometimes it would be interesting to talk with likeminded men who enjoy that same desires and full filment as I do. However, not everyone is of the same mind set and they have their own desires and may be ambitions. It all adds to the critical points, 'how far do I go?' and 'future years' with regard to your personal thoughts. More importantly is the effect it will have on 'others in my life!'

Chapter 13

Others in my life

O f the most important part of this book I've written, this chapter I believe needs some careful consideration. If you're single, have no family or even friends and colleagues, then it will be of little use reading further, however I believe that in most cases and speak generally for men who are married, live with partners or have some close relationship with another person, this needs a lot of thought before applying any actions.

As you'll see, I'm writing with Italic text and my feelings at present could not be stronger toward my desires to dress up in my clothes. The thought of them! The feeling of the material against my skin! The look of me as I appear in the mirror, the sensation of walking in high heels, the fragrances of makeup and the feel of hair on my shoulders would be wonderful, however circumstances today don't permit me to dress. There's no point in getting frustrated over these feelings as for certain, it will happen when the time is right.

This means that I have to take the opportunity when it arises and for that I mean, when it's in a relaxed atmosphere and everything around me including the people that I love and respect are happy for me to dress. If not, the whole sensation for me becomes false, not one I can really enjoy as I know there is something or, somebody not happy with my desire. Yes, I have feelings for others just as they have for me. The last thing on my mind would be to hurt anyone as a result of even my strongest desire to dress, it simply wouldn't be worth it.

One thing that I would also like to explain is the fact that again, I'm not in any way trying to convince anyone including wives, lovers, partners or whomever that after you've read my book, you should change your mind and support your man's desire to dress and let him get on with it. Wrong, it's certainly not what I want to achieve. What I felt right from that early age is the fact that somehow, done with discretion, perhaps supported and with limitations, then perhaps people may understand that it's not all bad news.

"My big strong man is now a sissy dressing in frilly knickers!!" Just because of a few square feet of material, some elastic and rib with a few meters of cotton thrown in, does the fact that the Big Strong Man is now some whimpering feeble soul? No, definitely not and to be honest, I would thing if he had the opportunity to share these feelings and be listened to without fear or prejudiced, then that man would actually become even stronger and more determined than ever.

There is no need try and analyses every facet of a man's mind, it's a complex piece of machinery and there are some wonderfully clever people who are charged with this task and, still have no definitive answer of how and why the mind works as it does. Will there ever be an answer? Somehow I doubt it and for good reason as we are all different and what real good would it to be able to put someone's mind and thought process in a box? In most cases, a boy is born a boy and girl is born a girl and each like different colours and toys, each have different voices and features and, that's our human race, male and female. As they grow, there are bound to be curious thoughts and fascinations of why one is different from the other and, what's wrong with that? At some point when questions are asked, children need good solid answers in order that they can understand the rights and wrongs of life, it's a fundamental part of growing up. They remember these points for the rest of their life and it helps as they grow older when making decisions of gender choice and how this could affect their future. It is at this point that people, male and female now freely have a choice to live as they wish and again, I'm neither supporting nor condemning the way of life chosen, what I will express is my opinion and from there, the affect it will have on others if we chose to step out of the norm.

You've read about me dressing in the evenings when my wife is with me and must be thinking, either she's a little different condoning such behavior or, quite by magic she doesn't mind that her strong man dresses up in ladies underwear. How wrong you are. It's been a subject between us that's caused both worries, concern and for certain, upset.

When I was explaining about me feelings and desires toward using makeup and a hair piece, I foolishly did this without mentioning the subject to my wife and, I made a big mistake. My curiously somehow got the better of me and I chose to 'go it alone' and have a try *or that was how I perceived it to be in my simple mind at that time. The house was empty and what harm could it do? This was a selfish thought as I gave little or no consideration toward her feelings and emotions if, she where to find out and she did!*

Dressed for the first time in 'my entire splendor' or, that's how I perceived myself and then the door opened and my wife came in. Shocked and horrified, she thought that the house was being burgled and that some strange woman had broken in. She screamed with horror! How stupid was that? I call myself a responsible man and always consider others and their thoughts and feeling yet, the one person closest to me in this world, I chose to deceive and frighten! Believe me, the thrills of makeup and all of the other items I was wearing soon slid away like dirty water down a wash basin plug hole!

It took a few minutes for me to explain "it's me!" and she didn't believe me at first for fear of perhaps being attached, molested or some other not nice act. When she did eventually realize it was me, she was shocked beyond belief! It was the sort of shock that took her breath away and it took some minutes before she could come to terms with her ordeal that 'clever me', had put her through. When someone you adore is treated in such away, it really makes you realize how silly, how stupid you are and posse's the question, "why did you do that?"

As usual with her wonderful approach to any situation, she is very quick to see positives and move things in the right direction, she's always been like that and I think more so in the years of being a mother, it's her natural way of making things right and for the best reasons. Within in minutes, the shower was running and speaking to me as though I was a naughty seven year old boy who'd done something really bad and was covered in dirt as a result of his wrong doings, she pointed me in the direction of the hot running water and said "don't come out until you've scrubbed that lot off you silly, stupid man!" By this time I was reduced to tears and felt the slow but horrible feeling of regret coming over me and was wondering what would be the fate of my actions.

The very last thing on my mind was to ever hurt her, to shock her and bring perhaps doubt in her mind as to our trust and relationship which we both treasure so much. Yet, I'd stepped over the line and that trust had been damaged by me. Proud, no far from it, in fact totally ashamed in every sense of the word! The clothes and wig all came off and the hot water with lots of soap washed away that person, that creature down the drain and the clothes went in the bin! My cheap makeup and other bits and pieces all joined them in the same place! That person was gone, gone and wouldn't ever return. The shame I felt for days, weeks and months after left some deep scares within me and sorry, is a very easy, cheap and convenient word. It doesn't go far when you have offended someone so stupidly, as I had.

Was I to bring the subject up and try and explain about it, or to best leave it and try with all will and effort along with time to see if this wound would heal? I couldn't begin to even think of all of thoughts that must have been going through her mind that day and, for many days after as knowing she'd found me than, she must have asked herself how often does he do this and, how long has it been going on? The seed of doubt must have been planted and that's the beginning of the end for many.

Probably that was one of the most stressful and worrying time within our married life and all brought on by me. I foolishly thought when alone sometimes, "what was all the fuss?" about I wonder as after all it was only me! Again, how foolish of me to even think like that without giving a though for her feelings. It took me quite some time to come to terms with some rational of why a lady would react in such a fashion, why does this seem to upset her so much and what really makes them to dislike this subject so much? Many questions came to my mind and as usual, it's only through research and constantly asking the question "why" was I able to bring some answers and start to shed some light on the subject.

For certain and going back to how I have described the fact that if a man dresses in ladies clothes, then regardless of the motive [other than a part in the local theatrical play] then he's stepping out of the box and moving toward the 'unknown'. He's immediately associated as man who's looking for some sex extension, something that he's deprived of and wants more, perhaps something new, perhaps something that only another man can provide. Can you start to begin to imagine how my wife must have felt in the after math of finding me all dressed up? It must have devastated her in many ways including her as my partner, lover and everything else as for certain, she must have thought to herself, "what did I do wrong and what didn't I do that made him want to dress in ladies clothes?" All of those precious times spent together, was it all lie, was it all show and was it all false? Are but a few of the questions that must have come to her mind and all brought on by me! How clever is that?

Occasionally as time moved on I'd bring the subject up briefly only to say I was sorry. This whole stupid affair was caused by me, however being the wonderful lady that she is, she never once brought the subject up or wanted to hold a grudge and argue over the whole affair. What was done was done and it can't be automatically righted overnight, it takes time and effort for open wounds to heal a little, the scars of which never totally disappear. My whole desire and feeling toward wanting to dress again seemed to take a very backward piece of my mind and for years, when the feelings and desires would arise, with all of my mind and willpower I'd try as hard as possible to 'delete' them as I felt they could only bring about more harm than good.

The lack of my understanding was partly to blame for my actions and it is for this reason I would recommend to any man who's dressing without his partners or wife's knowledge to stop and give some consideration for the consequences. Equally if you're contemplating wanting to dress and feel that you'll never be found out, be aware that if you make a mistake and it comes to the surface regardless of how silly it may seem, if leads to planting that seem of doubt in a relationship, stop and think twice before going any further. My actions in hind sight [and isn't that what all the clever people say] where totally selfish. I was thinking only of me and my desires, my feelings and didn't give a minutes thought toward my wife. What I didn't think about it, my immediate thoughts where, what could perhaps she find wrong with me in ladies clothes, after all ladies wear overalls and all of the men's work wear in this day and age of equality, they are only clothes.

Many things I over looked and one really important one was the fact I was introducing some stranger into our lives, our wonderful married life together! Yes a total stranger who appears in ladies clothes and would have to be accommodated in our home. That's not something to be taken lightly as the opposite applies, how would I like it if another women where to appear and live with us? It may sound silly be it true, and something that never crossed my mind for all the tea in China. It would compromise our relationship as "who would I be this particular day or evening?" would I be him or her? The term Jackal and Hide comes to mind and while it sounds silly the dual personality is starting to appear which can be a scary thought!

By now you're probably thinking, this guy's making too much of this subject, as it's only really pulling on a pair of knickers from time to time and what's the big deal in that? Remember, it's not only you but others around you and their thoughts count immensely!

My favourite French style satin knickers

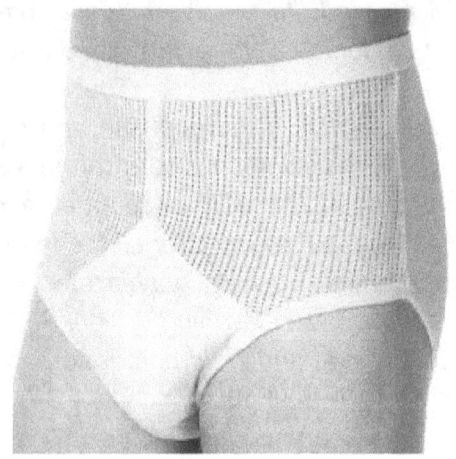

My favourite M&S cotton underpants

Chapter 14

Future years

*T*he future is something we all look forward too and, it's an opportunity for us to make dreams come true, to full fill promises and try and live up to our expectations. Then, reality strikes and the demands of everyday life step in an often divert those future plans by either delaying them, or causing you to live differently. More often than not, disappointments arise due to raising one's expectations beyond a reasonable level, they become too difficult to achieve and as a result are often cancelled with the tag "just too hard to do" attached to them.

We've plans for our future years which, we've worked towards and for certain, are realistic and will bring us both all that we desire in life. Looking back at me personally, I'm an extremely lucky man having been blessed with this inner most feeling for my desires to dress in ladies clothes and perhaps more so, to have contained them to a reasonable level and respecting others around me. When I say others around me, only one person knows of my desire, and that's my wonderful wife, as for the rest they have no incline of my feelings toward this subject. That being said given the heart ache and even unpleasantness it could cause if, my feelings where to be made public, then with respect for them I've kept it a very, "closed subject".

It's been a difficult choice to share my feelings with my wife as for certain in trying to explain to her why and how, there's a tendency to think I'm only doing this to convince her that it's "OK" and there's nothing to worry about. Without bringing the whole subject up and sharing my feelings and thoughts, then how else would I be able to explain them to her? One part of me has always thought that I'm loading her with something that she doesn't need to know, however if she's to understand me, my feelings, my desires and general wellbeing then, just as I'm there for her I chose to bring this whole subject out in the open.

Has it pleased her, no definitely not however I do believe now and after reading / editing this book she now has a better understanding of this unanswerable condition. It is unanswerable, the question of why just seems to bring even more questions and discussions. For me, I've realized my limitations, realized how far I want to go and been brave enough to talk about them all. Is she shocked by my feelings, yes I think she is as perhaps while she'd suspected that I had a liking for ladies clothes, she'd not realized how much I like different clothes and can describe them in detail. Wearing stocking and a girdle for instance is just pure delight when the feelings are with me, when they're not they couldn't be more uninteresting!

Time is a wonderful 'thing' as it brings more opportunity for us to look back at what has happened in life and, it makes us wiser for future judgments. Perhaps I was wrong to open this subject up with my wife, as it's brought some "grey hairs and sleepless nights" as she says! It's brought a few for me too, and the nights I've spent thinking about it all are countless, too many years to mention. Yes on one side it's brought about a level of comfort and satisfaction knowing that I have these unique feelings, however in knowing 'what to do with them' has been a challenge.

It could be said or argued if anyone wants to try and analyses my story that really, when all said and done I've brought no harm to anyone. In this I mean, I've not committed an offence and, been honest enough with myself *to bring out with a great deal of consideration my inner most feelings and thoughts to share with you. That's not an easy thing to do as for certain, just go back and read not only the previous chapters in this book, and in other books. Admission that you're a little different takes some guts, as you're actually prepared to let others know you're inner most thoughts. People usually keep these under wraps for years, often for a life time. Life is too short for that, it's a very precious gift and we have to look after, respect it and, make the most of it. I hope that when my "final moments" arrive, I've no regrets and left nothing unopened or undone! Leaving this earth that day and, hopefully going to a better place, I'd like to think I've done no one any harm, I've helped people, I've been a good citizen and 'done my bit to help others less fortunate then myself.*

Will I continue to want to dress in ladies clothes in coming years? I've asked myself this question in recent years and at present, yes I'd like to. Do I have any ambitions to go any further; no I've reached a point of contentment and satisfaction and realized my limitations, limitations of, how far I want to go and, what brings simple a pleasure. I doubt that my wife will ever reach a point of acceptance of my dressing, that's not something I will try and influence. She has her thoughts and I respect those just as she respects mine. Perhaps she may become more tolerant of seeing me dressed in underwear, if not that I'll have to curtail my dressing.

On many occasions, I've bought some piece of underwear and worn it from time to time quietly, discretely and then when my feelings have disappeared, I've chosen to dispose of them and felt better for it! Somehow, I felt that perhaps that was the last time and this whole subject would disappear, leave me forever and never return. A day, a week, month year it's never even crossed my mind then one

143

day, it reappears like some sort of pleasant rash [if there is such a thing?], as though it had never gone away and was just lay there waiting for me. So difficult to describe, I've often thought if I was ever to sit down and verbally go through this whole subject with a qualified person, they would think I'm a 'nut-case!'

There sometimes when I know with the wonderful sense of humour my wife has that she'd say something like, "you seams are crocked!" or "one's a bit bigger than the other!" however it's something which may, or may not happen. Making light of the whole subject I believe could bring a lot more contentment and happiness for a lot of men with the hope, that this would rub off and result in more care, more respect and more love and help for their wife or partner. May be one day she will tell me to stop, no more! Somehow I don't think she will as while it's not been a long time since bring this to her full knowledge, she's realized that I'm a happier and more contented person for this. Yes, I was contented before, but somehow now I feel that my life is really complete in knowing I can dress when the circumstance permit and enjoy those feelings I've explained to you.

One thing is for certain, I'll never abuse her tolerance, when I say abuse I mean all of a sudden announce that I want to go out dressed up or join a club! Those things that would cause her upset and shock. I will ask her opinion as I purchase some more clothes though nothing that will come as a surprise to her. What I'm looking forward to is the ultimate for me and my dressing habits, to be able to when the time is right wonder freely around the house in the clothes I chose and enjoy evenings in were we are both relaxed with my looks.

The question of bringing another person into the house has often crossed my mind and my wife has mentioned this. For

144

any wife or partner to be confronted with a 'third person' must come as a huge shock. At one time, my wife used to call me 'Shirl' and I honestly thought it was because she knew about my liking for ladies clothes and just used it a term of affection. I actually liked the name and really felt comfortable with the idea, however when I explained that this is how I interpreted it when explaining my desires and wanting to dress with her knowledge and consent, she said it was just a name she used for me, one amongst many. I've thought about asking if we can use that term when I feel the need and desire to dress by saying "I've got my Shirl feelings" so that she's aware of what I'm thinking. Let's see how this goes, however one thing is for certain I'd not be comfortable with me changing my name when the occasion arises for instance, "call me Diana!"

On the other side of the coin so to speak, if she said why not go out dressed one day, let's go and stay somewhere where, no one would know us and you can put on your outfit and we can go for a walk, go into town and even have dinner out, I don't know that I'd actually like that as it would mean stepping out, something that's never really appealed and, it would take a pluck of courage to make happen. You're probably thinking that's wish full thinking on my belief and by stating some of these things when she reads this book she'll automatically think well that's what he wants to do, so I'll support him. Wrong!

I've more of liking these days for older style girdles and would like to make a collection to wear, not spending a fortune and using every occasion possible to look for them, but simply as I find one on Ebay or in some high street shop to buy it, have it cleaned and enjoy wearing it from time to time with all of my other clothes. Lace up corsets are a wonderfully fascinating garment and I really enjoy drawing in my waist and the laces become tighter, the feeling is wonderful and the results are even more pleasing. I would ask, is there anything wrong in doing this in the privacy of our home? Having a draw full of underwear and the freedom to pull something out and try it on is wonderful privilege and perhaps the envy of many men.

My book is intended for all to read and for you to make of it what you will. If you're a worried wife and concerned that perhaps your husband is may be seeing someone else or, has some strange sexual fantasies as you've found a pair of knickers and a bra tucked away in an unusual place and know for a fact they they're not yours then, may be my explanation will help you have the conversation which is necessary to bring out in the open between you both that has perhaps been festering for quite some time. It doesn't automatically mean you agree with what he's telling you and, heaven knows what he's up to until he explains. If it's like me, just a fantasy, a feeling, a desire to wear ladies clothes and you can be sure, that's all it is, then maybe, maybe it's worth talking to him about it and hearing what he has to say.

Again I would stress to any man, can you imagine what a lady, would think finding a big pair of boobs in the draw that you'd forgotten to hide! It would frighten even the most tolerable and understanding partner to death! Don't forget, for you these may seem a fun thing, to a woman they are part of their body, a part which they treat very seriously and share with you from time to time. Finding a pair of 'substitutes', well would that make her feel insignificant? I certainly think so. Be considerate and put others feelings before your own.

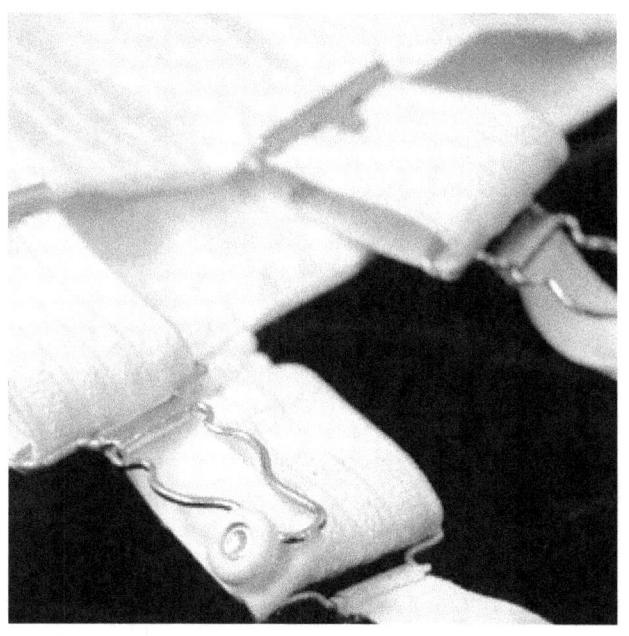

Chapter 15

Thank you

There is a saying "behind every good man is a good Lady" and I can certainly agree with that! Sharing my life with my wife is something which has been and still is a wonderful experience and we are happy two young kids just starting out on their live together! I wouldn't change it for the world and, if I had to do it all again, it would be with her as for certain, she is somebody very special. Giving me everything she possibly could and more, she never tires of finding the next 'thing to give'.

We share our good times which are nearly every day, from the time we rise until the moments when we drift off to sleep, and for this I really believe her wisdom in making me aware of how important it is to enjoy the moment and 'live for today' has been such a bonus for me. We do have our lows from time to time but generally these don't last long as they are usually disappointments beyond our control and this just a way of life. Not everything is easy and, we shouldn't expect that all will be given without being earned. Society today seems to think it owes them a living and a many other materialistic aspect of this world, however the feeling of having earned what you have bought and paid for is a delight and something everyone should gain satisfaction from.

We have made many sacrifices over the years for what we have believed was the betterment of each other, our lives, our future and the future for our children and grandchildren. It's good fun, we have many old fashioned virtues and values and these will never change. Of the most serious of offences we've ever committed between us are speeding tickets doing forty three in a thirty area and, for letting a parking ticket expire and forgetting the time! This starts to give you an understanding very briefly of the type of person I am and my wonderful wife is. I say this because she is not part of my writing of this book, however if it wasn't for her care, patients, understanding and love, I'd not have been able to even start to have drafted this book.

It came as a surprise to me when I asked her, "would you mind if I bought a few clothes?" that day when we were off shopping. She said, "No, I don't mind at all". Having this new found freedom has brought a new and what I believe is the final dimension to my desires and feelings toward dressing and for this, I am saying, "THANK YOU my love".

I know now she knows how important this is to me and, she realizes that for me to write a book on the subject has really brought the whole thing 'out in the open' for me. When I say out in the open, I mean from that early age, out between us and no one else.

Tolerance, patients, understanding, seeing the other person's point of view, respecting others are some of the advice I would give to any genuine man who's considering wanting to dress in ladies clothes even, if it's only to have a simple 'try on of some lacy knickers'. The results can be very satisfying, even more than the actual desire and feelings, *trust me!*